The Tsar and the President
Alexander II and Abraham Lincoln
Liberator and Emancipator

Edited by Marilyn Pfeifer Swezey

The Oshkosh Public Museum, Oshkosh, Wisconsin
July 12 – October 12, 2008

The Kansas City Union Station Museum, Kansas City, Missouri
November 1, 2008 – April 19, 2009

D1518911

Presented by
The American-Russian Cultural Cooperation Foundation

This catalogue accompanies the exhibition

The Tsar and the President:
Alexander II and Abraham Lincoln

State Historical Museum, Moscow
State Museum-Preserve "Tsarskoye Selo," Saint Petersburg
State Archive of the Russian Federation, Moscow
Library of Congress
Abraham Lincoln Library and Museum at Lincoln Memorial University,
Harrogate, Tennessee
National Park Service, Ford's Theatre National Historic Site
Lincoln College Museum, Lincoln, Illinois
The State Museum of Pennsylvania, PA Historical and Museum Commission
McLellan Lincoln Collection, John Hay Library, Brown University
United States National Slavery Museum
Erie County Historical Society, Erie, PA
Seward House Museum, Auburn, NY
Silver Swan Company

Private collections of:
Raymond F. Piper
The Hon. James W. Symington
Lacey R. Greer, Treasures of Imperial Russia

Sponsors:
Donald M. Kendall
Access Industries, Inc.
The Lee and Juliet Folger Fund
J.E. Robert Companies
The Trust for Mutual Understanding
Teresa & H. John Heinz III Charitable Fund
McLarty Companies

Published by the American-Russian Cultural Cooperation Foundation

Table of Contents

Acknowledgements

Organized by the American-Russian Cultural Cooperation Foundation. Founded in 1992 by a group of distinguished Americans, the American-Russian Cultural Cooperation Foundation engages in the support of increased cultural exchanges between the United States and Russia.

U.S. Organizing Committee:
ARCCF Board of Directors

Chairman of the Board
The Hon. James W. Symington

Joseph D. Duffey
Michael B. Goldstein
George Hambleton
Donald M. Kendall
Paul Rodzianko
Rabbi Arthur Schneier
The Hon. Jane DeGraff Sloat
Shelley M. Zeiger

Executive Director: *Alexander P. Potemkin*

Concept and structure of the Exhibition: *Marilyn P. Swezey, Reid Buckley*

Project Manager: *Reid Buckley*

Guest Curator (for the Alexander II portion of the exhibition) and Catalogue Editor: *Marilyn P. Swezey*

Guest Curator (for the Abraham Lincoln portion of the exhibition): *Alexa D. Potter*

Registrar: *Lee Williams*

Designer: *Reid Buckley*

Catalogue design: *Ellen Cornett, Graphic Design & Production*

Catalogue printing: *Gray Graphics Corporation*

Translators: *Dudley Hagen, Alexandra Draggeim*

Special thanks to: Nikolay Babushok, Natalia Montvilova, Natalia Potemkina, John Sellers of the Library of Congress, Lucinda Shaw, Paul Renard, catalog consultant

Russian Organizing Commitee:
Vladimir P. Kozlov, Chief of the Federal Archival Service
Sergey V. Mironenko, *Director of the State Archive of the Russian Federation*
E.L. Lunacharskiy, *Deputy Director of the State Archive of the Russian Federation*
L.A. Rogovaya, *Deputy Director of the State Archive of the Russian Federation*
Ivan R. Sautov, *Director of the State Museum-Preserve "Tsarskoye Selo"*
Larisa V. Bardovskaya, *Deputy Director of the State Museum-Preserve "Tsarskoye Selo"*
Iraida K. Bott, *Deputy Director of the State Museum-Preserve "Tsarskoye Selo"*
Alexander I. Shkurko, *Director General of the State Historical Museum*
Tamara G. Igumnova, *Deputy Director of the State Historical Museum*
Mikhail E. Koltsov, *Deputy Director of the State Historical Museum*
Konstantin K. Provalov, *Director of the History and Records Dept., Ministry of Foreign Affairs of the Russian Federation*
Elena V. Belevich, *Deputy of the History and Records Dept., Ministry of Foreign Affairs of the Russian Federation*
Irina V. Popova, *Head of the Archive of Foreign Affairs of the Russian Empire, Ministry of Foreign Affairs of the Russian Federation*
O. Yu. Volkova, *Curator of the Archive of Foreign Affairs of the Russian Empire, Ministry of Foreign Affairs of the Russian Federation*

Russian Coordinators: *Sergey P. Balan, Ludmila M. Kanaeva, Etery T. Tsuladze*

The following participated in preparing the Exhibition:
From the Russian State Historical Museum: *Andrei Yanovskiy, Svetlana Katina, Ludmila Maslova, Vera Kalachinskaya, Irina N. Khristyuk, Vladimir Okounkov, Georgi Sapozhnikov, Etery T. Tsuladze*
From the State Museum-Preserve "Tsarskoye Selo": *Alexandra D. Belyaevskya, Tatiana F. Bulgakova, Elena A. Eremeyeva, Irina I. Zaytseva, Tatiana S. Ivanchenkova, Elena O. Kalugina, Ludmila M. Kanaeva, Victoria F. Plaude, Aleksey S. Rogatnev, Tatiana V. Serpinskaya, Ekaterina N. Shvigleva, Victoria E. Elman*
From the State Archive of the Russian Federation: *Elena V. Aniskina, Sergey P. Balan, Elena A. Chirkova, Vladimir S. Glebov, Larisa V. Kryachkova, Irina V. Petrova, Victoria A. Zakirova, Irina N. Zasypkina*

The Tsar and the President:
Alexander II and Abraham Lincoln

It is particularly appropriate in our time to have a deep and comparative look at these two leaders on the eastern and western fringes of European civilization. Both men had to deal with extraordinary problems up until they were assassinated.

The parallels between Abraham Lincoln and Alexander II include the near simultaneous emancipation of slaves in the United States and the enserfed peasantry in Russia, the continuing eastward expansion of the Russian frontier and the westward expansion of the American frontier (something that the Library of Congress has been examining with our bilingual Web site, *Meeting of the Frontiers,* that has put nearly a million items of history from both countries on line), and the tumultuous problems of internal turmoil and war that haunted both of these reformist leaders.

The least noticed parallel theme is that Alexander's Russia, in a certain sense, faced a civil war at the same time as Lincoln's America did. It was the first "war of terrorism" against a modern state. Beginning with the attempt on Alexander II's life in 1866 until the final successful attempt in 1881, there was an accelerating war against the very existence of the Russian state. This war was conducted by young and radical students for whom expectations rose faster than the capacity for gratifying them in the tsarist system.

The violence in Russia was far less destructive of human life on a massive scale than was the American Civil War. But it psychologically permeated all aspects of Russian society and was immortalized in its early stages by what may still be the greatest political novel ever written, Dostoevsky's *The Possessed.*

The violence in Russia was tragically directed against the most far-reaching reformer ever to be tsar. Alexander II was, like Lincoln, a man of considerable vision and courage although not nearly as profound a thinker or as skilled a leader. One of the last perpetrators of an attempted assassination of a tsar was Vladimir Lenin's older brother, Alexander, who tried to kill Alexander II's successor and was in many ways a role model for Lenin. Assassinations of government officials at all levels of the Russian empire were the most sustained attempt of a small minority to destabilize a strong existing government. By the mid-1870s, the professional revolutionaries in Russia had gelled into the first organized human body in history to adopt the word "terrorist" as a badge of pride.

Lincoln faced far more massive internal violence, but Alexander II faced a form of violence that penetrated the consciousness of his society. His successor Alexander III and the even weaker Nicholas II who followed him, were unable to avoid the double blows of internal revolutionary opposition and external wars. Thus, the society that Alexander II presided over did not develop in the way envisaged by his early reforms. By contrast, Lincoln was able not merely to survive the far greater violence of the American Civil War, but to preserve the institutions of popular government and inspire the nation with a unifying vision.

The role of Lincoln is increasingly respected throughout the world. I was particularly moved when the Emperor Akihito of Japan, on a visit to the Library of Congress, asked to see the original copy of the Gettysburg Address. As the last major world leader still designated as an emperor, he quietly read out those final words about a government of the people, by the people, and for the people not perishing from the earth.

Alexander II, too, has a continuing appeal within Russia. I had occasion to ask both Mikhail Gorbachev in the late Soviet period and Vladimir Putin shortly after he became president, who was their role model among earlier Russian rulers. They both mentioned Alexander II.

It is particularly good for an American audience to become acquainted with this contemporary of Lincoln, and to have an opportunity to learn about the generally friendly relations that prevailed between our two countries until the Bolshevik Revolution. As our two nations strive to find a constructive relationship once more in the twenty-first century, we can be grateful for the good work of James Symington and his American-Russian Cultural Cooperation Foundation for making this exhibit possible.

James H. Billington
The Librarian of Congress

Foreword

To the dismay of Russia's powerful nobility, Tsar Alexander II on February 19, 1861 signed the Manifesto proclaiming freedom for the nation's 20 million serfs, thereby earning his sobriquet, "Liberator". In that same year he sent a message to President Lincoln expressing his hope that America would survive its civil crisis intact. Two years later in the midst of our Civil War Lincoln signed the Emancipation Proclamation as the first step in the journey to freedom of America's eleven million slaves which was to be completed by the 13th amendment to our Constitution adopted by Congress on December 18, 1865.

The historical parallels that link the lives, achievements and fates of President Abraham Lincoln and Tsar Alexander II of Russia have received scant attention from historians of both countries. The virtually simultaneous initiatives of the two leaders to rid their societies of the curses of serfdom and slavery are alone worthy of examination. But the solicitude which the Tsar expressed for the survival of our Union is a page missing from our textbooks.

The situation facing our newly elected President in 1861 was bleak enough without the prospect of hostile intervention by two of Europe's three Great Powers...Britain and France. It was the refusal of the third, Russia, to go along that aborted any such initiative. In this connection we can note that in the other defining crisis in our history, our War of Independence, Russia's Catherine the Great made an equivalent contribution to our survival by refusing George III's request for 20,000 Cossacks to help put down the rebellion in his American colonies. Republican threats to monarchy were presumed to be a shared concern. But Catherine drafted a polite "No", citing other demands on her time and attention and also her prescient apprehension of the difficulties her soldiery would encounter in a land so distant and so foreign in culture and clime.

For Russia to have played, albeit passively, such welcome roles at both the creation and preservation of our Republic would seem to warrant at least a footnote to history. It is the hope of our Foundation that this exhibit might help fill the gap; not as a footnote, but a visual text, albeit imperfect and incomplete, which could stimulate additional academic consideration and a keener public awareness of a defining moment in the history of human bondage and a Russian-American relationship that has endured the vicissitudes of two turbulent centuries.

So it is with warm thanks to both Russian and American contributors, that we submit the results of their valued insights and labors to the public.

James W. Symington
Chairman of the Board
American-Russian Cultural
Cooperation Foundation

Introduction

The American-Russian Cultural Cooperation Foundation is proud to present this exhibition to the American public. Dedicated to the Bicentennial of Abraham Lincoln, "The Tsar and the President" is focused on the finest period in the history of American-Russian relations. It is probably the most ambitious project within the framework of the Foundation's program of commemorating the common historical heritage of both nations. The Foundation has already celebrated successfully, the 175th Anniversary of Grand Duke Alexis' Goodwill Mission to the United States and the 200th anniversary of the creation of the Russian-American Company with major exhibitions. The Foundation has also observed the 50th and 60th anniversaries of the joint victory in the Second World War and the Bicentennial of U.S.-Russian diplomatic relations with celebratory events. "The Tsar and the President: Alexander II and Abraham Lincoln," (Liberator and Emancipator) continues this tradition.

We believe it might be of interest to American visitors to learn more about the unique parallels in the history of both countries and about a Tsar who had an amicable attitude towards the U.S., exchanged warm letters with Abraham Lincoln, and was his virtual ally in times of turmoil. This Tsar, who earned prominence in Russia as "The Last Great Tsar", instructed his Minister in Washington with this astute observation: "You should always remember that the best friend of Russia is the American people".

Historical events not only stimulated a friendly relationship between these two leaders, but also brought together the best elements of Russian and American societies of that time. Russians struggling against serfdom keenly followed the actions of the abolition movement in the U.S. Harriett Beecher Stowe's book, *Uncle Tom's Cabin*, was translated into Russian only a year after being published and was received with great interest by the educated Russian public. Americans were less familiar with the strong movement in Russia against serfdom, but works by the most vigorous Russian writers against serfdom, including the poems of Alexander Pushkin and stories by Ivan Turgenev and Leo Tolstoy, were to appear in the U.S. as well,.

The Foundation is proud to have initiated and arranged the erection of a statue commemorating Alexander Pushkin in Washington, D.C. and is currently participating in the creation of a monument in Moscow to Walt Whitman, Lincoln's contemporary and author of "O Captain! My Captain!", which was translated and well-received in Russia. These two statues can be said to symbolize the parallel attitude in Russia and America against bondage and oppression.

Our exhibition exemplifies the continuation of this spirit, which was renewed so vividly during the Second World War. I would also like to emphasize that this exhibition itself is the result of a joint Russian-American effort. It consists of objects generously provided by Russian and American lenders. During the preparation of the exhibition, Russian and American museum professionals worked together harmoniously to make this project happen.

This exhibition adds an important international dimension to the celebration of the Bicentennial of President Lincoln in the U.S., and we are pleased that it has been endorsed by the Abraham Lincoln Bicentennial Commission.

We hope that the exhibition will expand visitors' knowledge about an important period in American history as well as the history of U.S.-Russian relations and will contribute to better understanding and trust between our two nations.

Alexander Potemkin
Executive Director
American-Russian Cultural
Cooperation Foundation

Emperor Alexander II

1818-1881

17 April 1818	Born in the Nicholas Palace, Moscow Kremlin
14 December 1825	Became heir to the throne on the accession of his father, Nicholas I
17 April 1834	Ceremony of the Oath of Loyalty to Emperor Nicholas I
16 April 1841	Married Princess Maximiliana-Wilhemina-Augusta-Sophia-Marie of Hesse-Darmstadt(1824-1880), Grand Duchess Marie Alexandrovna
18 February 1855	Acceded to the throne on the death of his father, Nicholas I
20 February 1855	Wrote an introductory letter to President Buchanan
26 August 1856	Coronation of Alexander II and Marie Alexandrovna in the Uspensky Cathedral of the Moscow Kremlin
September 1860	First letter to President Lincoln
19 February 1861	Manifesto of Alexander II on the abolition of serfdom
1864-1865	New law on institutions of local self government, reform of the legal and court system, reform of the military court system
12 April 1865	Death of his son and heir, Tsarevich Nicholas Alexandrovich, of tubercular meningitis in Nice
16 April 1866	First assassination attempt on the life of Alexander II; saved from a nihilist's bullet by a liberated serf
June 1866	Naval mission of Gustavus V. Fox, to Russia
30 March 1867	Sale of Alaska and the Aleutian Islands (Russian America) to the United States for $7,200,000
20 November 1871	Grand Duke Alexis, son of Alexander II, arrives in New York for a 3 month official visit
1 March 1881	Assassinated by a terrorist bomb at the age of 63

Abraham Lincoln

1809-1865

12 February 1809	Born Harden County, Kentucky
1828	Lincoln observes a slave auction in New Orleans
1831	Moves to New Salem, Illinois; works as a clerk in the general store
1833	Serves as county surveyor and postmaster
1836	Receives his law license
1837	Settles in Springfield, Illinois
4 November 1842	Marries Mary Todd
16 June 1858	Nominated as Republican senator from Illinois
6 November 1860	Elected 16th president of the United States
20 December 1860	South Carolina secedes from the Union, followed by Mississippi, Florida, Alabama, Georgia, Louisiana and Texas
12 April 1861	Confederates open fire on Fort Sumter, marking the beginning of the Civil War
1 January 1863	President Lincoln issues the final Emancipation Proclamation freeing all slaves in territories held by Confederates
24 September 1863	Russian naval vessels arrive in New York; several days later another squadron arrives in San Francisco. They remain for seven months.
19 November 1863	Delivers the Gettysburg Address at a ceremony dedicating the battlefield as a national cemetery
8 November 1864	Abraham Lincoln is re-elected president
9 April 1865	General Robert E. Lee surrenders to Gen. Ulysses S. Grant at Appomattox Court House in Virginia
14 April 1865	Shot by John Wilkes Booth at Ford's Theatre, Washington, DC; dies early the next morning

Framed photograph of Alexander II in his study in the Winter Palace
St. Petersburg, 1870s
Frame: wood, metal, velvet
State Museum-Preserve "Tsarskoye Selo"

The Tsar and the President
A Meeting in Diplomacy

Marilyn Pfeifer Swezey

t was a most unlikely connection – a friendly alliance between the vast Russian Empire celebrating its millennium and the new, young American Republic not yet one hundred years old. The two systems of government were diametrically opposed.

One was an autocracy ruled by an hereditary monarchy and the other, a democracy led by an elected president. Further, the elegant persona of the Tsar, Alexander II, was in complete contrast to the lanky, homespun figure of the President, Abraham Lincoln. The two figures side by side would have been quite an unusual picture if they had ever actually met, though they ultimately shared a tragic fate.

They corresponded, however, and there they met on the equal footing of good diplomatic rhetoric. Six letters from Alexander II to President Lincoln can be seen in the National Archives of the United States, each written in two languages, French and Russian, and signed "Your good friend, Alexander". Also preserved in the National Archives are hand copies of Lincoln's replies; included is one of his handwritten drafts with words crossed out. It is signed, "Your good friend, A. Lincoln".

Portrait of Alexander II
Watercolor
Alois Gustav Rockstuhl
State Museum-Preserve
"Tsarskoye Selo"

Alexander II was a well educated man. He spoke four languages, including English, and was tutored from birth to assume the "burden of power" of a nation considering itself to be the

Portrait of Grand Duke Paul Alexandrovich
Watercolor
Ivan Kramskoy, 1870
State Museum-Preserve "Tsarskoye Selo"

Grand Duke Paul, seen here at the age of ten, was the youngest son of Alexander II. He would later suffer the same tragic fate as his father. In 1919 he was imprisoned by the Bolsheviks and executed in the Peter and Paul Fortress.

successor to the Byzantine Empire. The roots of Russia went back a thousand years, a milestone that Alexander II would officially observe in 1862. He was 37 when he ascended the Russian throne. He was "tall and very handsome", in the words of the American Minister to St. Petersburg at the time, "with grey eyes and auburn hair".

The Tsar had long been fascinated with America. It began in his childhood when the great Siberian missionary to Alaska, Father Ioann Veniaminov, visited the Winter Palace. He captivated the young Grand Dukes, sons of Nicholas I, with the stories of his experiences in the Russian colony in North America. [Father Ioann later became head of the Russian Orthodox Church (Metropolitan Innokenty) in recognition of his remarkable accomplishments in Russian America.]

Abraham Lincoln was born and raised in a log cabin in rural Kentucky. He was a self educated man, nine years older than Alexander - tall and gangly, and (self-professed) not a handsome man. His rise to the presidency of the United States through the chaotic politics of the American electoral system of that time was a remarkable phenomenon. He seemed to come out of nowhere. And indeed, there were many among the Washington political and social set at that time, including the Russian Minister to Washington, Edouard de Stoeckl, who had their doubts about the "provincial lawyer from Illinois". It was a paradoxical alliance brought about by an unexpected turn of events and the mutual international interests of the two nations.

Diplomatic relations between Russia and the United States had been established early in the 19th century, soon after the birth of the American nation. The first Russian Consul to America, Andrei Dashkov, arrived in Philadelphia on July 1, 1809. On November 5th of the same year, John Quincy Adams, the future American president, presented his credentials in St. Petersburg to the Tsar, Alexander I. Russian diplomats at that time were instructed, along with their usual diplomatic tasks, "to study the traditions and customs of the country of their residence, to encourage active and deliberate trade and to develop mutually beneficial relations between both countries". This last and perhaps most important instruction was to come to fruition during the time of the Lincoln presidency and the American Civil War.

The story begins in 1855. Alexander II inherited the patrimony of his father and was crowned Emperor, "Tsar of All the Russias". Among his first official communications was a letter to the President of the United States – Buchanan, not yet Lincoln – expressing the hope that he "would be given the same consideration that was extended to his father", Nicholas I. The Tsar's first letter to President Lincoln is dated September 21, 1860, just a few months after Lincoln's inauguration. It is a friendly, almost familial, announcement of the birth of his son, Grand Duke Paul Alexandrovich. There are altogether twenty-one letters of Alexander II to Presidents of the United States in the National Archives.

An important appointment at the beginning of the Tsar's reign was Prince Alexander Gorchakov as Chancellor and Foreign Minister. He was an eminent statesman and scholar of history – a man whose respect for the United States was great. "The American Union," he declared, "has exhibited to the world the spectacle of a prosperity without example in the annals of history".

Gorchakov became the Tsar's right hand man in foreign affairs and proved to be quite instrumental in the Tsar's policy toward the United

Portrait of Prince Alexander M. Gorchakov
Oil on canvas
I.P. Keller-Villiandi, 1867
State Historical Museum, Moscow

A real entente cordiale developed between the Russian autocracy and the American democracy – a "mutually beneficial" and supportive relationship, between the Tsar and the President, Alexander II and Abraham Lincoln. The period of their relationship was not long, barely a decade, based on the years of the

Portrait-badge with miniatures of Emperors Alexander II and Alexander III
Russia, 2nd half of the 19th century
Gold, silver, diamonds, quartz, glass, tempera, painting
State Historical Museum, Moscow

This high imperial award is thought to have belonged to Prince Gorchakov, who received such a rare double-portrait badge on his retirement from service to the two emperors.

States. The regular letters of Edouard de Stoeckl from Washington kept Gorchakov fully informed on events in the nation's capital. Gorchakov showed these letters to Alexander and his replies often carried the tsar's handwritten affirmation, in one case "Bravo!".

Lincoln presidency, plus a few additional years in its wake. The reign of Alexander II was much longer, extending from 1855 until his assassination in 1881. But the events that were orchestrated during those years – the Tsar's support of the Union, the visit of the Russian fleet in 1863, the Fox delegation to Russia in 1866, the sale of Alaska in 1867 and the visit of Grand Duke Alexis to the United States in 1871-72 – had a lasting effect on the history of both nations. Today, the Tsar and the President stand parallel in their great accomplishment of reform and in the tragic fate which they both shared as a result.

Diplomatic Excursion of de Stoeckl and Seward to Saratoga Springs,
August 1863
Photographer unknown
Albumen print on photographic paper
Seward House Museum, Auburn, NY

During his many years of service in the United States, the Russian envoy Edouard de Stoeckl, and Secretary of State, William Seward, became great friends and often traveled together. They are pictured here with a large entourage of foreign dignitaries during a summer excursion to the popular resort at Saratoga Springs, New York. It was just one month before the arrival of the Russian fleet in New York.

From left to right, front row: Frances (Fanny) Seward (Seward's daughter), William H. Seward, Ellen Perry (family friend) and Baron Gerolt (Prussia); Back row: Mr. Sheffield (Attache, British Legation), Lord Lyons (British Minister), Mr. Mercier (French Minister), Baron de Stoeckl (Russian Minister), Mr. Molena (Nicaraguan Minister), Mr.Schleiden (Hanseatic Minister), Mr. Bertenatti (Italian Minister) and Mr. Bodisco (Russian Legation).

Façade of the Grand Palace, Tsarskoye Selo
V. Sadovnikov, 1860s
Watercolor
State Museum-Preserve "Tsarskoye Selo"

Tsarskoye Selo, the Tsar's village, began as a small estate given by Peter the Great to his wife, Catherine, in 1710. The Grand Palace was commissioned by their daughter, Empress Elizabeth, and is known today as the Catherine Palace, in honor of Elizabeth's mother. Designed by the Italian architect, Bartolomeo Rastrelli in the 1750s, the building extends one thousand feet in length. It was the site of official receptions and military reviews for all succeeding Romanov rulers when in residence at Tsarskoye Selo, located fifteen miles south of St. Petersburg.

Alexander II, Tsar-Liberator

Andrei Yanovsky

He would have been a wonderful ruler in a well-organized country and in peaceful times, when preserving the order would be all that was required. But he is not blessed with the character traits of a reformer.

A.F. Tyutcheva . Diary. 1856

 n Wednesday of Easter week, April 17 (29), 1818, Alexander, the first child of Grand Duke Nicholas Pavlovich, and his spouse Alexandra Feodorovna, the Prussian- born Princess Frederica Louise Charlotte Wilhelmina Caroline, was born in Moscow. His arrival in this world was marked by a 201 cannon salute and the exalted poetry of V.A. Zhukovsky. Several days later, Grand Duke Alexander Nikolaevich, carefully wrapped in lacy infant wrapping, was appointed chief of the Hussar Life Guard Regiment, one of the most elite divisions of the Russian army.

All of seven and a half years passed and young Alexander received a highly responsible addition to his title of Grand Duke – "heir and tsarevich." On December 14 (26), 1825, his father became, as fate had willed, Emperor Nicholas I within a single hour, and he brought his rosy-cheeked heir into the large courtyard of the Winter Palace, where the Life Guards Engineering Battalion was standing. Quickly dressed by a valet in the child's uniform of a Hussar cornet, the child was frightened to death by the thundering "hurrahs" of the powerful and strong-voiced, mustached Hussars and began to cry loudly.

22 years went by… Having faithfully completed a military course under the supervision of Karl Karlovich Merder, an experienced veteran officer, the Tsarevich was awarded the rank of full general. However, Alexander Nicholaevich's primary mentor and educator during all this time was the

View of the Kremlin toward the Spassky Gate
Engraving from the watercolor by G.M. Lori
Early 19th century
State Historical Museum, Moscow

The Nicholas Palace, where Alexander II was born, can be seen at left, above the landscaping inside the fence.

great Romantic poet and close friend of Pushkin, Vasily Andreevich Zhukovsky, one of the most brilliant men of the XIX century, who put humanity, morality, and virtue above any sort of education. Nevertheless, the future sovereign received a thorough and well-rounded education: he had command of four languages, mastered the basics of natural and exact sciences. He had a good understanding of history, logics, philosophy, geography, and ethnography. Finally, he was an excellent musician, skilled in drawing and rhetoric. Considerable

attention was also paid to Alexander Nicholaevich's athletic development: he achieved extraordinary success in riding, fenced easily, swam fast, and loved doing gymnastics.

Emperor Nicholas I took great care to make sure that his son would become a "statesman-like and military man." He used all means to include his heir in parades, reviews, and government affairs. From the beginning of the 1840s, Alexander participated in affairs of the State Council and the Senate as well as on various

Portrait of Tsarevich Alexander Nikolaevich
Watercolor
P.F. Sokolov, 1829
State Archive of the Russian Federation, Moscow

This sensitive portrait of the eleven year old heir reveals some of the qualities noted in the character reference written by his tutor, Karl Merder several years later, in 1833:
"Exceptionally sound mind comprehending everything correctly, if not always quickly, and retaining whatever contains a sensible idea for a long time."

lawmaking, state construction, finances, and foreign policy. The future monarch was educated better and more thoroughly than his father. Young Alexander was noted for his common sense, quick eye, and tenacious memory. In his disposition, he was more flexible and much less stubborn and uncompromising than Nicholas I.

At noon on February 18 (March 2), 1855, Emperor Nicholas Pavlovich Romanov passed away in the Winter Palace in St. Petersburg in the 59th year of his life. Just before his death, he sadly confessed to the successor standing at his bedside: "I am handing command over to

Portrait of Grand Duchess Alexandra Feodorovna, mother of Grand Duke Alexander Nikolaevich, the future Alexander II
Oil on canvas
Alexander Molinari, ca 1810
State Historical Museum, Moscow

higher committees and commissions. In 1846 and 1848, he chaired two secret committees dealing with the issue of serfdom. Having audited, in his youth, a course of lectures given by the outstanding politician Mikhail Mikhailovich Speransky, the tsarevich had a rather solid grasp of the problems of justice and

Room in the Nicholas Palace of the Kremlin where Grand Duke Alexander Nicholaevich was born
Watercolor from the original by P. Zaitsev, 1836
State Historical Museum, Moscow

10

Portrait of Grand Duke Nicholas Pavlovich, the future Nicholas I, father of Grand Duke Alexander Nicholaevich
Oil on canvas
Unknown artist, from the original by O.A. Kiprenski, mid-19th century
State Historical Museum, Moscow

in inevitable defeat, finally devastated the country and put it on the verge of a financial disaster. The degree of peasant unrest against serfdom increased noticeably, and, although almost all of it was of a disorganized and spontaneous nature, clouds of "new Pugachev-style riots" were ominously looming on the political horizon. The "intellectual ferment" was engulfing

Portrait of Karl K. Merder
Watercolor
M. Gradovskaya, from the original, 1834
State Historical Museum, Moscow

Merder, tutor of Alexander II, wrote in a character report of his young charge in 1833: "…His rather pronounced courage and decisiveness reach the level of fearlessness, which gives me a pleasant hope of seeing him, in due time, as a courageous and decisive man who is unflappable in the face of danger and prepared for anything…

you, but the state of affairs is not what I desired. I am leaving you with much to be concerned about and much to be worked on." Then, collecting his last strength, the dying sovereign added, staring straight at his son: "Hold on to everything. Hold on to everything!" This phrase was accompanied by an energetic hand gesture that meant that he must have a tight grip. But it was precisely this last wish of Nicholas I that was the most difficult to fulfill.

By the spring of 1855, the glory and power of the Russian empire was far behind the historical horizon. The Crimean War, threatening to end

Portrait of Vassily Andreevich Zhukovsky
Lithograph
A.I. Lebedev, from the original by F. Kruger, 1869
State Historical Museum, Moscow

Zhukovsky, the famed 19th century Russian poet, was the main tutor of Alexander II.

an increasingly greater part of the educated public, which was dissatisfied with the military-style police regime of Nicholas I. Russian authority on the world stage, which had been unquestionable not too long before this, plummeted. Bureaucrats – from the minister and senator down to the last desk clerk and scribe – were up to their ears in bribery and embezzlement. An overpowering crisis was jarring the seemingly indestructible edifice of the state system, which Nicholas I had erected carefully,

brick by brick, over the course of his almost 30-year reign. As a surprise to many, cracks started running through its mighty structure, and it began to collapse in front of their very eyes. It became clear to everyone that the empire built by Nicholas I had turned out to be a "Colossus on Clay Legs."

The existing situation clearly required that very decisive and urgent measures be taken by the power of the autocracy. All eyes were turned with hope in the direction of the new monarch, who, having acceded to the throne, had neither his own program nor any clear-cut political views. He was not prone to liberal ideas, nor did he attempt to carry out any strict reactionary measures. The foundation of his world outlook was clearly the stability of the monarchy in Russia. Although, in the opinion of those close to the young emperor who knew him well, he was no less a conservative than his father, Alexander II set out to find new solutions and new people in the name of preserving the autocracy. Already within a year, he understood that it would be much better and safer for the government to initiate reforms "from above," rather than wait until they come "from below." Thus, beginning in 1857, the country entered into a period of preparation and structuring of bourgeois reforms that included all aspects of public life. The abolition of serfdom in 1861 inevitably led to reforms in the areas of local government and justice, education and press, finances, and military affairs.

This extraordinary time brought a multitude of distinguished personalities to the forefront of government activities, including Grand Duke Konstantin Nicholaevich, the brothers N.A. and D.A. Milyutin who were representatives of the liberal bureaucracy, and dozens of others. These people sincerely believed in the possibility of bringing Russian society to a new level of historical development peacefully and without

Portrait of Alexander II
Oil on canvas
Ivan Tyurin, 1874
State Museum-Preserve "Tsarskoye Selo"

Reading of the Manifesto on the liberation of peasants at a landowner's estate
Chromolithograph, V.F. Timm, 1861
State Historical Museum, Moscow

social upheaval. The emperor himself believed in such an outcome.

The well known historian and researcher of the "Age of the Great Reforms," L.G. Zakharova, professor on the History Faculty of Moscow University, states correctly that "in his world outlook, character and temperament, Alexander II was not a reformer. He became one by virtue of circumstances, lacking the capabilities and qualities of a prominent states-

Portrait of Grand Duke Konstantin Nikolaevich
Oil on canvas
Unknown artist, 1850s
State Historical Museum, Moscow

Grand Duke Konstantin, younger brother of Alexander II, was his close adviser and a strong supporter of the liberation of the serfs.

man. In the main activity of his reign – abolishing serfdom and the reforms of the 60s and 70s – he took as his basis a liberal framework for large-scale national reforms and general reorganization, at the same time, facing the facts of a harsh military defeat (the Crimean War) and general discontent in the country. However, not being himself a liberal by conviction, in the end he subordinated the carrying out of this transformation to the interests of preserving the autocracy, erroneously equating it with the interests of Russia."

This fatal error led Alexander II to a tragic outcome. Radical revolutionary forces which, by virtue of the "Great Reforms," were at large within the broad national expanse, "executed" the Tsar-Liberator on March 1 (13), 1881 precisely because he considered the main goal of his life and reign, and the objective to which he directed all of his reforming activity, to be the preservation and further strengthening of the institution of autocratic government in Russia.

The prominent Russian historian, V.O. Klyuchevksy, who was born the year Alexander II was married (1841) and died the year that the 50th anniversary of the abolition of serfdom was celebrated (1911), presented a surprisingly accurate and astute understanding of the mysterious and deeply tragic nature of the Tsar-Reformer. In his last scholarly article, he wrote: "Alexander II inherited a legacy weighed down by belated reform issues, promises that had been long overdue, and recent excruciating losses… Emperor Alexander II had to force through his reforms … He differed noticeably from his most recent predecessors, as he lacked the tendency to play the role of tsar… Whenever possible, he was just himself in an everyday manner as at leisure. He spoke naturally, using words that first occurred to him without worrying about the impression he would create. He acted as he saw fit at the given moment without thinking too much about the consequences. He did not wish to appear better than he was, and he was frequently better than he appeared to be."

Portrait of Empress Marie Alexandrovna, wife of Alexander II
Oil on canvas
T.A. Neff, 1864, after the portrait by Winterhalter
State Historical Museum, Moscow

Born Princess Maximiliana-Wilhemina-Augusta-Sophia-Marie of Hesse-Darmstadt, she became Grand Duchess Marie Alexandrovna on her conversion to the Orthodox Church and marriage to the heir to the Russian throne.

Accession to Power and the Coronation

Ludmila Kanaeva

t the time of Alexander II's ascent to the throne, Russia had been an empire for 133 years. Peter the Great had adopted the title of emperor on October 22, 1722 and from that time on, Russia was known as the Russian Empire. Earlier that year, Peter had issued a "Decree on the Inheritance of the Throne", naming his successor. The decree remained in effect until the end of the 18th century, when Paul I changed the rule on the day of his coronation, April 5, 1797, issuing a decree establishing the inheritance of the throne by the eldest son of the reigning emperor. The proclamation that was declared with each new emperor's reign, also named his successor, who assumed the title of tsarevich.

Based on the 1797 law, which fixed the order of succession, the members of the Imperial house swore oaths of fealty to the sovereign and to the Fatherland on reaching the age of sixteen. The oath had two parts, one being a general civil oath and the other dedicated to the inheritance of the throne. Taking the oath was a pledge to observe the rules governing inheritance of imperial power and family order as established by the 1797 law. General Mikhail Speransky, a prominent statesman whom Nicholas I had entrusted with preparing Grand Duke Alexander, the future Alexander II, for this important ceremony, saw the oath as a reinforcement of the law, since conscience and the judgment of God were the only things that could bind an autocrat to observe it. "The oath is a confession of conscience and religion," Speransky held, "calling God as a witness to the faithfulness of the promise and subjecting him who swears it, to God's anger and vengeance if the oath is broken."

The oath took place at the Winter Palace in a ceremony attended by the imperial family, the court and guests. Following a prayer service in the Great Palace Church, the emperor led his heir to the church lectern, upon which lay the cross and the Gospel. There the tsarevich pronounced the state oath. The imperial regalia – crown, orb and scepter – were displayed round about the lectern.

The military oath took place before the cross and the Gospel in St. George's hall, the Throne room, which held the banners of the guards regiments. The oath-taking was an important state occasion, formally proclaimed in a published document and the text of the oath, with the signature of the tsarevich, was entrusted to the state archives.

On February 18, 1855, Grand Duke, Tsarevich, Alexander Nicholaevich, ascended the throne, succeeding his father on the day of his death. On the following day, Alexander was proclaimed emperor at the Winter Palace, and a prayer service was held in the Great Palace Church.

An emperor's ascent to the throne culminated in the coronation, through which the church consecrated the emperor's power. Known as the Holy Coronation, this was a ceremony consisting of the crowning, anointment with holy

Ceremonial entry of Alexander II into Moscow on Tverskaya Boulevard for the coronation
Oil on canvas
Unknown artist
State Historical Museum, Moscow

oil, and the recited prayer of the emperor for strength and wisdom in "his great service" of governing for the welfare of the people. The day of the coronation was a national holiday, as decreed by Peter the Great in 1721, to be celebrated along with the tsar's birthdays and names days.

The coronation of Alexander II was held in the ancient capital of Moscow, according to the tradition. The ceremony and its accompanying celebrations were particularly grand and splendid. The solemnities began on August 17, 1856 with the tsar's festive entry into Moscow, which had been carefully prepared for the event. This could be felt in the mood of its inhabitants and the festive look of its streets and squares. "I was astonished by the traffic in the streets," recalled Count G. A. Miloradovich, "the crowd and the expectant attitude, especially among the common people. There was noise inside the Kremlin from the work going on in preparation for the illumination of the entire Kremlin, the bell tower of Ivan the Great, etc. The walls and towers of the Kremlin were draped in nets right to the top, the dome of the bell tower was turned into a crown, a ring of archways was thrown up around Theater Square in the city, and the university was decked in crests, monograms, and other decorations for the upcoming illumination, as were the houses of Count Sheremetyev and the Governor General."

The program of celebrations was extensive and varied: balls and a masquerade in the Kremlin palace, a ceremonial presentation at the Bolshoi, balls at the French and Austrian embassies and in the Assembly of the Nobility, a military parade, outdoor merrymaking at Khodynka field, and much more. But the outstanding events of those days were Alexander II's solemn entry into Moscow and the coronation in the Kremlin; these left an indelible impression on those who were present, and

some wrote vividly about all this in their memoirs. We will turn to those memoirs to "have a look" at those very interesting moments in history.

Alexander II's solemn entry into Moscow took place on August 17, 1856, although the entire imperial family had arrived in the capital several days earlier and taken up residence at the Petrovsky Palace. On the day of the entry ceremony "from early morning the entire population of Moscow crowded along the route, from the Petrovsky Gates right up to the Kremlin. Both sides of Tverskoy and Yamskoy were lined with forces in glittering uniforms. One of the officers of the Preobrazhensky regiment, deployed in the Kremlin, recalled: "While we were stopped, getting ready, and then taking positions on Red Square, I was able to observe what I believe reflected the grandeur of the celebration: it was a manifestation of the people's feeling, their spirit. The innumerable crowd filled all the space around the Kremlin as far as the eye could see. And still more and more huge groups kept pouring in from all parts of the city and its suburbs." The procession of the emperor and his family from the Petrovsky Palace to the Kremlin took place in bright, sunny weather. The sovereign, mounted on a gray steed, wore a general's uniform. He rode surrounded by his elder sons–Tsarevich Nicholas Alexandrovich and Grand Duke Alexander Alexandrovich–foreign monarchs, and a huge suite. After him followed ceremonial golden carriages. The widowed Empress Alexandra Feodorovna rode in one, the Empress Maria Alexandrovna and her son Vladimir in another. Grand Duchesses Maria Pavlovna, Alexandra Iosifovna, Elena Pavlovna, and Maria Nicholaevna rode in the two carriages that followed. The ringing of bells mingled with the firing of salutes and joyful cries. All the buildings along the procession route

Portrait of Metropolitan Filaret of Moscow in coronation vestments
Oil on canvas
N.E. Rachkov, 1857
State Historical Museum, Moscow

Then a salute was fired from a hundred and one cannons. All the churches began to ring their bells, and didn't stop all day."

All during the next three days heralds, accompanied by trumpeters and drummers, went around Moscow announcing the coronation of Emperor Alexander II and Empress Maria Alexandrovna to be held on August 26. Alexander II's coronation followed the same ceremonial protocol used by his father, Nicholas I. The prototype of this ceremonial had been established by Peter the Great, who introduced it for the coronation of his wife, Empress Ekaterina Alexeevna.

The coronation took place in the Uspensky Cathedral. There stood the throne of Grand Prince Ivan III, prepared for the new emperor; the throne of Tsar Mikhail Fedorovich, for the new empress, and the throne of Tsar Alexei Mikhailovich for the widowed Empress Alexandra Fedorovna. "As the sovereign came into the cathedral, Metropolitan Filaret addressed him," as described by A. F. Tyutcheva. "Then His Highness venerated the relics and icons before ascending the steps to the throne, where the widowed empress already awaited him. The entire imperial family, and foreign princes, stood at the foot of the throne … The ceremony began. The sovereign read out the Creed in a loud, firm voice that reached throughout the church … Complete silence fell everywhere as the metropolitan dressed the sovereign in the emperor's cape and regalia, and handed him the crown." The emperor himself placed the crown on his head, then took up the scepter and orb and sat upon the throne. Then he "called to the empress, who came and knelt before him. He first touched her forehead with his crown, and then placed on her head a small crown, which a lady-in-waiting fastened in place with diamond pins … Then the sovereign, on bended knee,

were draped in rugs and flowers. "After passing Tverskoy, the procession stopped at the Kremlin and turned right into the Spassky Gate. Here the sovereign set an example by following sacred custom and removing his helmet while he passed through the gates. The column halted at the Uspensky Cathedral, where the Moscow clergy, with Metropolitan Filaret at their head, awaited the imperial family. The emperor entered the cathedral and venerated the cross and the icons of the Savior and the Virgin of Vladimir. As the sovereign crossed the cathedral's threshold, Supreme Marshall Prince Golitsyn offered a solemn gift of bread and salt.

Emperor Alexander II in coronation robes
Chromolithograph from the original by an unknown
artist, 1850s
State Historical Museum, Moscow

Empress Marie Alexandrovna in coronation robes
Chromolithograph from the original by an unknown
artist, 1850s
State Historical Museum, Moscow

pronounced that marvelous prayer in which he
calls for God's help in carrying out the arduous
but noble task ahead. Then Filaret prayed aloud
while all except the sovereign remained on their
knees. A deacon loudly pronounced all the
emperor's titles, and called for God's blessing
on him. The choir sang a *Te Deum.*"

During the liturgy that followed, the imperial
couple was sacramentally anointed with holy
oil.

Then the solemn procession left the Uspensky
cathedral and proceeded to the other Kremlin

cathedrals, the Archangel and the
Annunciation. The emperor walked in front
wearing his crown of diamonds, with the orb
and scepter in his hands, under an awning carried by the court minister and several adjutant
generals. The empress, in her crown and man-
tle, walked beneath a second awning.

"At the sight of the awning beneath which the
crowned monarch walked," one witness
remembers, "the splendid, golden company
around him and the vast, motley crowd of the
common people were filled with the same joy
and emotion. The splendid light of the sun

Anointing of Emperor Alexander II by Metropolitan Filaret during the coronation ceremony in
the Uspensky Cathedral of the Moscow Kremlin, August 26, 1856
Lithograph
V.F. Timm 1856
State Historical Museum, Moscow

ignited that sea of brilliance, and all light culminated in the crown on the head of the emperor. It is difficult to describe the delight and rejoicing of the crowd, reaching to frenzy." After visiting the cathedrals the emperor and empress proceeded to the Kremlin Palace, and before going in they bowed to the people from the Red Staircase. Coronation day ended with a ceremonial banquet in the Granite Chamber.

The coronation celebrations in Moscow ended with a magnificent display of fireworks at Lefortovo field on September 17, 1856. The imperial family watched from the balcony of the Golovinsky palace. Here is how one eyewitness describes the spectacle: "The fireworks started off with a fiery ball from above, flying from the balcony to a basket of flowers, which together with the column supporting it turned suddenly into a rose bush. A bright-winged butterfly flew off towards the grove. After rockets of every description came another tableau: the monument to Ivan Susanin in Kostroma. At the

Festive procession of Emperor Alexander II through Ivanov Square in the Moscow Kremlin after the coronation in the Uspensky Cathedral
Oil on canvas
G. Schwartz, 1856
State Historical Museum, Moscow

Illumination of Moscow on the occasion of the accession to the throne of Alexander II, 1856
Watercolor
V. Sadovnikov, 1856
State Museum-Preserve "Tsarskoye Selo", St. Petersburg

same time, an air from *A Life for the Tsar* was played. The next tableau was the monument to Peter the Great in St. Petersburg. After that came the Narva Triumphal Arch, and when it appeared the national anthem thundered out, performed by 1,000 singers and 2,000 musicians. Cannon shots alternated with the roll of drums."

On September 18, 1856, Alexander II made a pilgrimage to the Troitsky-Sergiev monastery to venerate its holy relics. He then departed to St. Petersburg, entering the city on October 2, accompanied by his family and a resplendent entourage; the ceremony drew huge crowds of spectators. The procession halted at Kazan Cathedral, where a prayer service was conduct-

МОСКВА
1856. Г.

УЖИНЪ

La crème d'orge à la princesse,
kalte Schale.
L'aspic de sondac à la belle vue.
Les filets de gélinottes à l'Aspasie,
Truffes.
Les quenelles à l'indienne, aux
points d'asperges.
Les chapons, coqs de bois. Rôti.
Les melons d'eau, garnis d'une
macédoine de fruits au ma-
rasquin.

Menu of a gala dinner during the corona-
tion festivities in Moscow, September 2,
1856
Chromolithograph, Petersen's lithography shop, St. Petersburg, 1856
State Historical Museum, Moscow

ed in the emperor's presence, and then continued to the Winter Palace. "All during the procession, the voices of the people and the troops
flowed together in a single-hearted Hurrah!"
recalls one of those who took part.

A splendid ball, given at the St. Petersburg
Assembly of the Nobility and attended by the
emperor and empress, concluded the celebration of Alexander II's ascent to the throne.

The Zubov Wing of the Grand Palace, Tsarskoye Selo
Luigi Premazzi, 1855
Watercolor
State Museum-Preserve "Tsarskoye Selo"

This addition to one side of the Grand Palace was commissioned by Catherine the Great in the late 18th century for her last favorite, Platon Zubov. It was designed in the neo-classical style that she favored by architects Velten and Neelov. The private apartments of Alexander II and his family were in this wing. It was their primary residence.

The Tsar's Special Attribute

T. F. Bulgakova

he imperial family always kept dogs, who were greatly loved and enjoyed truly "royal" privileges. Those who did not know Alexander II personally could recognize him by his beloved dog, always present alongside him. This fact was known in all St. Petersburg, and even in the distant provinces of Russia.

Favorites of the Emperor's family
Oil on canvas
Johann Schwabe, 1867
State Museum-Preserve "Tsarskoye Selo"

Watercolors by Eduard Hau, which hung in the imperial couple's rooms in the Catherine Palace, portray charming lapdogs sharing the leisure of their owners as full members of the family: they frolic, doze, and even pose for the artist. Emperor Alexander II adored his pets and commissioned pictures of them from noted artists. Shwabe's painting "Dog" (1845) and Randel's "Dogs of Alexander II" (1849) hung in Alexander's antechamber in the Zubov wing of the Catherine Palace until the time of the war. In the emperor's study was a sculpture of, "Alexander II, life size, wearing a greatcoat, with a dog lying at his feet." Unfortunately, none of these has survived.

Alexander II inherited his love for four-legged friends from Catherine the Great and from his father, Nicholas I. All through Alexander's life, dogs were his faithful companions. He almost never parted from them: he took them for walks, to concerts, and on journeys within Russia and abroad.

The life of a dog is not long, however, and one faithful friend would take the place of another. It may not be generally known that at Tsarskoe Selo, in addition to the famous dog cemetery of Catherine the Great, there is another in the "garden of Emperor Alexander I," and another on the Children's Island in the Alexander Park, where dogs belonging to the last Russian emperor are buried.

Among the archival documents at the Tsarskoe Selo museum is an inventory from 1918, which mentions four stones from the dog cemetery in the "garden of Emperor Alexander I." These, regrettably, have not been preserved to the present. Simple words cut into slabs of white marble speak eloquently of the feelings cherished by their august master for these friends, who served him faithfully and truly in this life. Nearly all of the inscriptions begin with the word "faithful." For example, "Faithful Mulya" was the inseparable companion of Alexander as tsarevich from 1833 to 1846, on his travels in Russia and to Germany, Italy, Holland, and England. From the long list of journeys undertaken by this stranger, we can see that he was very dear to the tsarevich, who could not stand to part with him even for a short while. "Faithful Rubi Mostik" was beside Alexander Nikolaevich from 1849 to 1858. One maid of honor at the court, A. Tyutcheva, recalls from 1855: "I had made soup for Mok, the Emperor's favorite Italian greyhound. When I picked up a crust to wet it in milk, the Emperor handed me another, saying: 'No, you always took this for Mok. For heaven's sake do not change anything of our good habits.'" Another dog is commemorated on a slab with inscriptions in Russian and French: "Faithful Punch: 1867-1875." Lidiya Ogloblina, daughter of the noted artist L. Lavrov, often saw the Emperor in Pavlovsk. "The Emperor always came on horseback, accompanied by one riding-master, and usually with his black setter Milord or red pointer Punch."

Among these pets the favorite was the above-mentioned black setter, Milord, whose master had his image recorded in painting and sculpture, as Catherine the Great had done for her beloved Zemira, an Italian greyhound. It was this black setter who became the tsar's special attribute—he is the animal most often mentioned in the memoirs of people who met the Emperor.

Although there were many superb animals among Alexander II's hunting pack, he favored Milord above all the rest. When the Emperor went hunting, it was Milord he most oftren took along. The writer L. Sabaneev gives a detailed description: "I saw the Emperor's black dog in Ilyinsk, after a dinner to which the sovereign had invited the directors of the Moscow

The Mirror Study of Empress Marie Alexandrovna in the Grand Palace,
Tsarskoye Selo
Watercolor
Edward Hau, 1860s
State Museum-Preserve "Tsarskoye Selo"

Alexander II and Marie Alexandrovna at home in the Zubov wing of the Grand Palace, two faithful friends resting nearby.
(to the rt. of the Emperor's chair)

hunt. It was a very large and exceptionally beautiful lapdog with a fine head, well dressed, but there was little of the setter in it: the legs were too long, and one leg was completely white. They say this setter was a present to the Emperor from some Polish grandee, and the rumor had it the dog was "not quite pure-bred." The dog's bloodline did not concern the emperor. He loved Milord for other qualities—gentleness, charm, and loyalty—and Milord fervently returned his love.

Those who encountered the tsar walking with his dog remember cheerful, sad, and sometimes curious episodes. There is a story about one school lad reduced to tears by Milord. The family of this boy had entrusted him with an important mission: to take his grandmother a name-day cake, whose ingredients were a family secret. In the importance of his task, the boy forgot totally that he often met the tsar, accompanied by his dog, in the Summer Garden. On meeting the tsar, he snapped to attention, saluting with his right hand and dropping his left, which held the cake. There was a sudden, strong tug at his left hand, and the precious burden was dropped. To the youngster's amazement and horror, he saw the cake lying in a puddle, and the tsar's dog tearing furiously at the paper and sinking greedy teeth into the treat, fragrant with saffron and almonds. Our hero burst into tears, muttering something at the dog. The tsar, seeing this, tried to persuade him not to cry, but apologize to his grandmother, saying it was all the tsar's fault for going out to walk with an underfed dog. All was settled by an officer coming from the Winter Palace to the boy's school, bringing a splendid confection from Kochkurov's for the grandmother as compensation for the spoiled cake, and several pounds of the best candy for the boy.

Curious citizens would make special trips to the Summer Garden or Tsarskoe Selo park to see the tsar, who would arrive in a carriage alone, but always with a shaggy black hunting dog. The following incident, with a university student, belongs to the genre of unexpected meetings with Emperor Alexander II. The young man and his friends, who had never seen the tsar, went to the Summer Garden hoping to catch sight of him. In front of them a tall officer, head wrapped in a *bashlyk*-style hood, was walking along the embankment arm-in-arm with a young lady. The young man darted up alongside the officer and bumped against his sword. The officer reprimanded the unruly youngster. Immediately after that, people in civilian clothes approached the group of students, asking what the Emperor had spoken to them about. The officer walking with the lady turned out to have been Alexander II; his companion was Grand Duchess Maria Alexandrovna, his daughter. The "terrible powers" took the young man back to his institute, where the director found it beyond belief that the students had not recognized the tsar: "But you saw the dog running along in front of him? All Petersburg knows that dog!"

Tsarskoe Selo was Alexander II's favorite residence. Here he could combine relaxation with work on important questions of state. In his minutes of leisure, he liked to walk with Milord around the big lake in the Catherine park. Here is what A. Bologovskaya, who was sometimes brought to play with the tsarevich, recalls about encounters with Milord. At their first meeting, the large black dog had jumped out of the bushes, barking, and frightened her terribly, but an officer (Alexander Nicholaevich) appeared suddenly to calm her. After that, she often met Alexander Nicholaevich in the shady alleys of

The Dressing Room of Tsarevich Alexander Nikolaevich in the Grand Palace,
Tsarskoye Selo
Watercolor
Edward Hau, 1850
State Museum-Preserve "Tsarskoye Selo"

Two of Alexander's dogs can be seen at large in the room. A servant in the traditional dress of the Court Arabs, is seen approaching at the doorway.

the park with Milord. Girl and dog became fast friends. She would bring sugar and cookies specially for Milord, and on seeing her Milord would rush towards her at full speed. Once he even knocked her into a ditch.

Milord lived a glorious dog's life, and he is mentioned more than any other in Alexander II's memoirs. The emperor hardly ever parted with his favorite, except for once, and that proved the dog's ruin. In 1867 Alexander was to travel to Paris for the World's Fair, and it cost his entourage no little effort to persuade him not to take his dog along. Alexander II ordered that Milord be left at Tsarskoe Selo, not suspecting that in doing so he was pronouncing a death sentence on his friend. Milord, pining for his master, stopped eating and died of a broken heart. By special order of the tsarevich, the dog's death was concealed from Alexander II until his return, since "an expression of grief on the face of the august guest … might be ascribed to concerns of a political character."

Another marble slab appeared in the dog cemetery at Tsarskoe Selo: "Gentlest and dearest, faithful Milord: 1860-1867."

The emperor's feeling of loss was so great that he commissioned a sculpture immortalizing Milord's image. The emperor is depicted in Hussar uniform, mounted on a horse. Alongside him lies Milord, in the same favorite position recorded in photographs. This bronze group was executed in 1870 by the famous sculptor Matvei Chizhov. Another composition was done in marble, also in 1870, by the sculptor I. Podorezov. In 1880, the noted painter Nikolai Sverchkov repeated Chizhov's subject in a portrait: "Emperor Alexander II on Horseback," which also depicted Milord.

After the loss of his black setter, Milord, Alexander Nicholaevich acquired another, equally beloved, friend—a Newfoundland, Milord, who went with the emperor to the Russo-Turkish war. This dog would also "play master" in the tsar's office at the Winter Palace, pressing against a button that sounded an alarm. The whole watch would come rushing in, to the tsar's astonishment. Milord also attended concerts. A contemporary recalls that once the great violinist Vinyavsky was playing in the tsar's presence. Evidently the performance pleased Milord; he got up from his usual place at the tsar's feet, went over to the musician, and stood up on his hind legs, resting his front paws on Vinyavsky's shoulders. Vinyavsky tried to ignore him and kept playing, but Milord would not leave him in peace, following the movements of the violinist's hand with his enormous snout. Finally the tsar, who had been watching with a smile, took pity and asked, "Is the dog bothering you, Vinyavsky?" The harried musician answered, "Your Imperial Majesty, I am afraid that I am bothering him." The tsar laughed and called the dog.

The tsar never forgot Milord. On February 19, 1880, on the twenty-fifth anniversary of his assuming the throne, Alexander was presented with a briefcase, which held among other things a picture of his favorite dog, painted by Benard.

No other Romanov emperor had such an original "special attribute" as Alexander II, who as one foreigner put it, was "a true sovereign in all his being."

Lincoln in Life

John Sellers

he life and career of Abraham Lincoln is the personification of "The American Dream": the widely accepted belief that poverty and the rural way of life promote character, and that hard work is the key to success in life. As Lincoln pointedly advised a young teacher and aspiring lawyer: "Work, work, work, is the main thing."

Lincoln's early life stands in stark contrast to that of Tsar Alexander II of Russia, and it is hard to imagine the two would have so much in common at life's end. The ancestry of Lincoln's mother, Nancy Hanks, cannot be traced with any assurance, for she was a bastard child. The legitimacy of Lincoln's own birth is without question, however, and yet it is hard to imagine a more humble beginning. Born on February 12, 1809 in Hardin County, KY, the second child of Thomas and Nancy Hanks Lincoln, the gangly baby bore little resemblance to his stocky parents. Then, as time would reveal, he deviated even further in his mental capacity. Although Thomas possessed the requisite skills for survival on the western frontier, he could neither read nor write, nor did he make any attempt to infuse his son with the desire for personal improvement.

A dreamer by nature, Thomas kept his small family on the move, first to Indiana, and then to Illinois, always in search of cheaper and more fertile farmland. Thomas was a subsistence farmer/hunter with little or no appreciation for his son's insatiable lust for learning. Thus Lincoln grew to manhood with less than a year of formal schooling, and that only in one-room schoolhouses with children of mixed age, nor did it deter him from ravenous reading. Lessons of the classics, Shakespeare, Pilgrim's Progress and the Bible were absorbed at every opportunity including sessions behind the plough. Legally independent at 21, Lincoln left home, seldom to return. But opportu-

Portrait of Abraham Lincoln
Mezzotint
William Edgar Marshall, Ticknor and Fields, Boston, 1866
Library of Congress

Lincoln's son, Robert Todd Lincoln, lauded Marshall's portrait for "its Excellence as a likeness" and French illustrator, Gustave Dore, declared it "the best engraving ever made by any artist living or dead."

nities were few, and he struggled and failed at various enterprises until he took up the study of law. The effort seemed to unleash a latent but superior intelligence, and he was soon jostling for position in the political arena. Success was not immediate, but come it did, and before long Lincoln was living in the new state capital of Springfield and thinking it was time to marry.

There are differences of opinion on whether cultivated Mary Todd settled upon Lincoln for a husband, but anyone familiar with their personalities would have identified Mary as the initiator. Unfortunately, it was not an ideal marriage, although their devotion to each other throughout their respective lives could not be questioned. Lincoln simply made the best of the situation by immersing himself in his law practice. Mary, meanwhile, kept house and bore four children, all boys, over a span of 10 years. Success followed Lincoln's almost total absorption with litigation. By the end of his 25-year practice, it was widely accepted that he was the best trial lawyer in the state of Illinois. Not that he was especially knowledgeable in the finer points of the law, for his strength lay in the art of persuasion. Few of Lincoln's peers could match his skill in eliciting a favorable verdict from the jurors.

Had not Stephen A. Douglas introduced legislation in the U.S. in 1854 to reorganize the Kansas-Nebraska Territory, opening the way for the introduction of slavery in a theretofore pro-

Lincoln's hammer
Wood, iron
ca. 1850-1865
Lincoln College Museum, Lincoln, Illinois

Forever tinkering, Lincoln kept a number of tools, including this hammer, in his desk at the White House.

hibited region, Lincoln might have lived out his life in relative comfort in his expanded home in Springfield, IL. Long an admirer of the Declaration of Independence, most notable the declaration that "all men are created equal," Lincoln was appalled. His opposition to slavery was long standing, but muted. The system of popular sovereignty advocated by Senator Douglas both perpetuated and expanded slavery. Suddenly, almost out of nowhere, Abraham Lincoln found his voice, and it was a shout against this abominable institution. Lincoln sounded the alarm across the state of Illinois, and after joining the newly created Republican Party, across the nation. His campaign for the U.S. Senate in 1858 was a continual condemnation of slavery. Although he lost to Douglas, he soon found himself speaking in cities like Chicago, Cincinnati, and even New York. The nation was listening, and their applause bolstered Lincoln's confidence. Having considered himself unfit for the highest office in the land, his aspirations and ambitions soared, and at the Republican Convention in Chicago in 1860, he won the nomination for President of the United States.

Victory for Lincoln in the Presidential contest of 1860 came at a cost. Eleven southern states eventually seceded from the Union in protest to the direction they perceived that the nation was taking on the issue of slavery. In most of these states, Lincoln's name was not even on the ballot. But win he did, albeit, with a minority of the votes cast. His speech at Springfield upon his departure for Washington in February 1861, reflects both the pain he felt over the momentous change in his life and his trepidation over the nation's future. Lincoln sought to avoid war with the Confederated southern states, but his determination to maintain the Union made it a foregone conclusion that there would be war. And the war came.

No American President suffered more during his term in office than did President Lincoln. As Lincoln once remarked to a friend during the darkest days of the Civil War, "If there is a worse place than hell, I am in it." How he bore the burden of so many deaths, even that of his most promising son Willie, is hard to imagine. He lost weight, and he slept little. Added to this, Mary, always an emotional woman, seemed unable to win the respect due the First

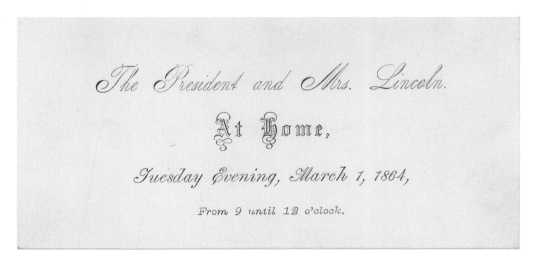

The President and Mrs. Lincoln at Home Calling Card
Paper, 1864
McLellan Lincoln Collection, John Hay Library, Brown University

Despite her best efforts, Mary Todd Lincoln failed to find her place in Washington society.

Lady. But she behaved badly at times, and there was little cause for celebration in the Lincoln White House.

During the first two years of the war, the Union Army was bested in battle after battle. However, the nation held together, and gradually incompetent generals and political appointees found their way to the rear, allowing talented military strategists like Ulysses S. Grant and William T. Sherman to assume command. The greater manpower and industrial might of the North began to take effect.

Even the purpose over which the North entered the war seemed to change. Although fundamentally a contest over slavery, northerners could not be induced to adopt such cause. They fought first to maintain the Union, and only secondarily to abolish slavery. But the lid was off a long simmering pot, and there was no way to put it back. Society itself was boiling over. In his great wisdom, Lincoln saw the opportunity to redirect the attention of the American people to principles upon which the nation was founded. We hear him even today in such landmark speeches as the Gettysburg Address, and the Second Inaugural Address.

In reflecting on the tragedy that befell Lincoln at the war's end, true victory may have come in death. The American people were so horrified, North and South, at Lincoln's assassination, that there could be no turning back. There have been setbacks, however temporary, but the future of the freedman is guaranteed. Who could think otherwise without bringing dishonor to the most beloved President in our history as a nation?

Pounce box
Wood, metal
Ca. 1847-1857
Abraham Lincoln Library and Museum at Lincoln Memorial University, Harrogate, TN

Lincoln wrote his letters, speeches and orders with a fountain pen. Shaking powder (generally made out of ash and ground cuttlefish bone) out of the pounce box helped dry the ink and keep it from smudging. Lincoln used this pounce box when appointing Stephen Harding as Governor of Utah Territory on March 31, 1862; having signed the document, he dried the ink and gave the box to Harding.

Travel Order for Major John Hay, with lithograph of Abraham Lincoln and Photograph of John Hay
Albumen print on paper; lithograph, handwritten note of A. Lincoln
Photograph of John Hay by Bierstadt Brothers, New Bedford, MA, ca. 1860
Collection of James W. Symington

"Washington, July 15, 1861
Major John Hay, my private secretary, goes to New York upon public business of importance. I desire that all necessary facilities
may be given to him in the matter of transportation.
A. Lincoln

The Naval Mission to Russia of Gustavus Vasa Fox

Edward Kasinec, with Robert H. Davis, Jr.

n 1863-64 the Russian fleet paid a well-received visit to New York and Washington. This visit was a watershed event in Russian-American relations. Not only was it seen as a tangible expression of Russia's support for the Union, it also provided an opportunity for the American people, both in person and via many newspaper accounts, to put a human face on a distant land. At whistle stops from New York to Niagara, the officers of the fleet were feted and praised for their unassuming, gentlemanly demeanour. It marked the occasion of the first Orthodox service held in New York, performed by the 'Russian Padre' of the fleet, a Dane named Nicholas Bjerring (d. 1900). It also re-kindled a lasting interest in Russia on the part of Anglican-Episcopal churchmen and laypeople, who continued their study of, and contact with, Russia long after the fleet departed.

In 1866, following the unsuccessful attempt on the life of 'Tsar-Liberator' Alexander II, and close on the heels of the murder of its own leader, the 'Great Emancipator', the United States Congress issued a declaration expressing relief that the life of the Tsar had been spared. The United States was also grateful that Russia's sympathies were with the north during the Civil War, in contrast to powers such as Great Britain that backed the vanquished Confederate States of America.

On the invitation of the Russian government, following the end of hostilities, the U.S. Federal government dispatched a reciprocal delegation, a naval mission to Russia, led by Gustavus Vasa Fox.

Sailors on the Russian frigate Osliaba, harbor of Alexandria, VA
Photograph
Andrew J. Russell, ca. 1863-64
Library of Congress

The Osliaba, one of the vessels of the Russian fleet that arrived in New York and San Francisco in September 1863, was visited by Mrs. Lincoln when it came to Alexandria. The ships remained in US harbors for seven months. The entire visit of the fleet was seen by the Lincoln administration as well as the general public, as a saving grace to the Union during the difficult days of the Civil War.

Who was Gustavus Vasa Fox? Born in 1821 in Saugus, Massachusetts, he studied at Phillips Academy in Andover, and received an appointment to Annapolis, the American equivalent of England's Royal Naval College at Greenwich.

Gustavus Vasa Fox
Photographic print on a carte de visite
St. Petersburg, photo by Levitsky, 1866
Library of Congress

This photograph was taken of Fox during his mission to Russia in 1866 by Levitsky, one of the official court photographers of Alexander II. He presented the Congressional Resolution "personally to the Emperor of Russia at one today" as he reported by cablegram from St. Petersburg on August 8, 1866. Prince Gorchakov, Chancellor, later reported to Stoeckl, the Russian Minister in Washington, that "The Emperor has been most favorably impressed with Mr. Fox. The tact with which he has acquitted himself of his mission has been highly appreciated in our official circles". For Fox, the visit was a joyful encounter with Russia and the Russians. "I was like a bee wandering among flowers," as he described it. "But The striking feature of our visit was the spontaneous reception everywhere accorded to us by the people themselves. The flag of the United States has been shown and honored for a thousand miles in the interior of Russia. . ."

The Great Russian Ball at the Grand Academy of Music, November 6, 1863
Wood engraving
Winslow Homer, Harper's Weekly, November 21, 1863
Collection of the American-Russian Cultural Cooperation Foundation

Soon after the arrival of the Russian Fleet to New York, a lavish ball was given at the Academy of Music on 14th Street in honor of the officers. Admiral Lisovski, Commander of the Russian Fleet, is reported to have protested against the extravagant expenditure of a ball during war time, but plans went forward nevertheless. As described in Harper's Weekly, it was attended by crowds of people who "streamed in incessantly, seriously, joyously – in all moods, manners and ways". The "upper proscenium boxes were draped in Russian and American flags" and "every lady had diamonds on". A lavish supper from Delmonico's was served in an adjoining hall and included "twelve thousand oysters, one thousand pounds of tenderloin, one hundred pyramids of pastry and three thousand five hundred bottles of wine".

After a fifteen-year naval career, Fox resigned his commission, marrying the daughter of a prominent New England judge and political figure, and became the brother-in-law of President Abraham Lincoln's Postmaster General. Before

Leroffeky and his captains.

Rear Admiral S. S. Lisovski and His Officers
Matthew Brady, ca. 1863-1864
Naval Historical Center

Admiral Lisovski, Commander of the Fleet is seen with the captains of the ships and Grand Duke Konstantin Nicholaevich, Admiral of the Imperial Navy and brother of Alexander II, who accompanied the fleet on its historic visit.

Pictured left to right: Captain Lieutenant P.A. Zelenoi of the Almaz; Captain First Rank I.I. Bytakov of the frigate Osliaba; Captain Fedorovsky of the frigate Alexander Nevsky; Rear Admiral Lisovski,; Grand Duke Konstantin Nicholaevich; Captain Lieutenant P.V. Kopitov of the frigate Peresviet; Captain Lieutenant R. A. Lund of the corvette Variag.

the Civil War, Fox was an investor in the Bay State Woolen Mills in Lawrence, Massachusetts. When South Carolina's Fort Sumter was encircled by secessionist volunteers in the waning days of the administration of President James Buchanan in 1857-1861, he left his business interests to serve his country, designing a plan to relieve the federal garrison. He presented it for consideration by the lame duck Buchanan, who promptly rejected it. He found a more receptive ear in the newly-inaugurated administration of President Lincoln, and was made Assistant Secretary of the Navy in August, 1861 under Gideon Welles (1801-1878). By many accounts, contemporary and historical, Fox called the shots for the navy during the Civil War, championing the appointment of Admiral David Farragut (1801-1870) to command the Union blockade of the Mississippi River, as well as the development of the then revolutionary technology of ironclad warships.

The Fox mission had a variety of purposes. First, it was, undoubtedly, a sincere expression of gratitude to Russia and its leader. Second, it provided an extended opportunity to view at first hand the human and material resources of European Russia. Third, it provided an opportunity to exchange views on trade, and specifically protectionism, which both Russia and the United States strongly supported. Finally, it permitted some preliminary face-to-face secret discussion of the future of Russian America, Alaska, which was purchased from Russia just a year later, in 1867.

For the Russians, too, the visit provided an opportunity to observe American ironclad technology at first hand, as one of Fox's flotilla was the 'Miantonomah', the first monitor to make a transatlantic crossing. Fox and his mission travelled to St. Petersburg and environs, Moscow, Nizhni Novgorod, Rybisnk, Uglich, Tver, and other European cities of the Empire. Like their counterparts from the Russian fleet in 1863-64, they were received with great fanfare everywhere they travelled.

The mission took place at a fascinating point in the histories of both the Russian Empire and the American Republic. Both had recently 'emancipated' large populations, and both were struggling to make the transition work. Both were moving from agricultural towards industrial economies. Both were nascent economic competitors, who sought trade protectionism as a means of developing their industrial bases. Both ruled over large territories and diverse populations, some of whom resisted this rule bitterly.

In the winter of 1866, following his return to the Untied States, Fox transferred to Secretary of State William Seward (served 1861-1869) eight historic documents on paper, given to him by a 'Mr. Pogodin, a distinguished citizen of Moscow' (that is, the historian and collector Mikhail Petrovich Pogodin, d. 1875), for deposit in 'some national institute or museum in Washington'. This cache, first brought to the attention of one of the authors by a colleague and literary scholar, Antonia Glasse of Ithaca, New York, included a letter from Peter the Great, a poem by Gavriil Derzhavin, with his corrections and remarks, a signed poem by Aleksandr Pushkin, and an autographed fragment of text by Nikolai Gogol. Deposited by Seward at the Smithsonian, these documents were kept in a 'table drawer in back room', according to Smithsonian accession records at the time.

The bulk of Fox's collection of 'Russian Souvenirs', however, stayed with his family until 1909, when 'the heirs of Mrs. Virginia L. W. Fox, his widow', bequeathed it to the Smithsonian, at that time referred to as the 'U.S. National Museum'. A study of this important

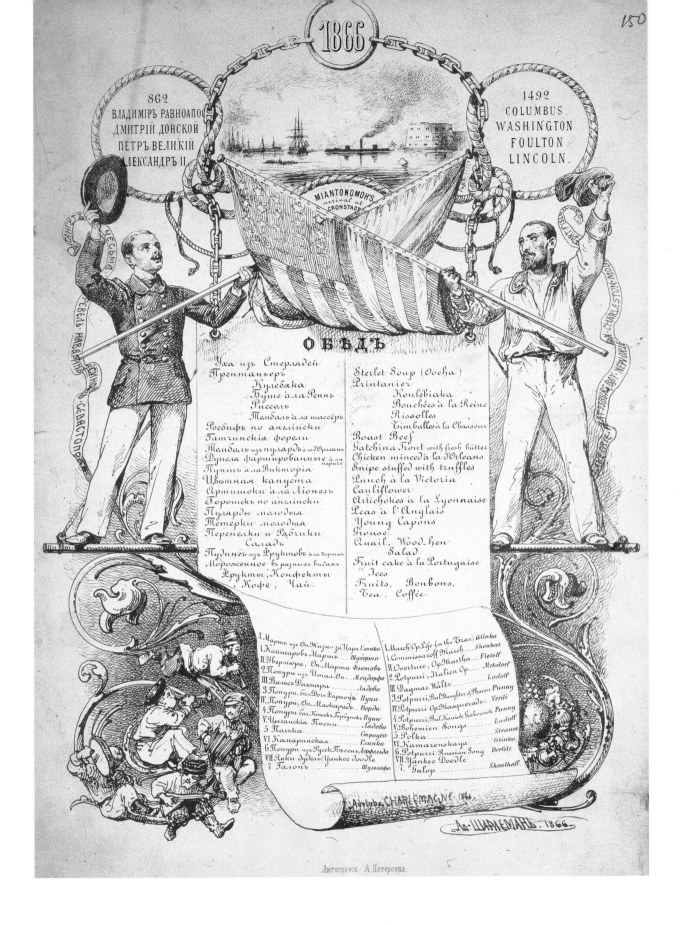

Menu of a Naval dinner at Kronstadt in honor of the arrival of the American delegation headed by Gustavus Fox in July 1866
Chromolithograph, A. I. Charlemagne
St. Petersburg, lithography shop of A. Petersen, July 28, 1866
In Russian, French and English State Historical Museum, Moscow

In honor of the arrival of the American delegation on July 26, 1866, a grand dinner was held on July 28 at the Naval Club at Kronstadt, reciprocating the warm reception given to the Russian sailors in America a few years before. Admiral Lisovski, by then Commandant at Kronstadt, came aboard the Miantonomah to welcome Fox.

This artistic menu which was designed for the occasion, illustrates the Miantonomah arriving in Kronstadt at the top. On each side of the image is a short, comparative time line of Russia, beginning in the year 862, and America, which was discovered in 1492. Following, are the names of important figures in the historical development of each country.

In Russian on the left side is written: "Vladimir Equal to the Apostles", referring to Prince Vladimir of Kiev who brought Christianity to Russia with the baptism of the citizens of Kiev in 966; "Dmitry Donskoi", the Moscow prince who led the first decisive victory over the invading Tatars in 1380; "Peter the Great", who declared Russia an empire in 1722; and "Alexander II", who initiated the Great Reforms, including the liberation of the serfs, in 1861.

The American side, in English, lists: "Columbus", as discoverer of America; "Washington", as the first president; "Foulton", as inventor of the steam boat; and "Lincoln", the counterpart to Alexander II, with the emancipation of the slaves in America.

The menu, written in both languages, includes dishes popular in the Russian and American cuisines, such as "Koulibiaka" and "Roast Beef". The musical program, seen below the menu, includes "Yankee Doodle".

collection of diplomatic gifts and isolated ephemera is a unique 'time-capsule' of nineteenth-century diplomacy, revealing what images Imperial Russia sought to project to a foreign observer and what, in turn, engaged the interest of a savvy American diplomat.

This collection consists of a small number of diplomatic gifts, some quite remarkable, from the Tsar and his government. Unquestionably the most striking of these is a Siberian green malachite chest that contained Fox's certificate of honorary citizenship of St. Petersburg, inlaid with gilt bronze and the arms of the city. A gold snuffbox, probably made by the Court jeweler Ludvig Breitfuss (d. 1868) was presented to Fox by Alexander II with thirty-two diamonds and a miniature of the Tsar. It is a remarkable piece. Other gifts came from the other end of the socio-economic spectrum, including a peasant carved wood and metal model of a monument erected in honor of the delegation in Cherepovets in Novgorod province. The collection also includes silver trays, salt cellars, and a striking gold and cloisonné snuffbox, presented by various esteemed citizens encountered on the journey.

There are also many important presentation volumes, including: the remarkable chromolithographic 'elephant-size folio' coronation album of Alexander II; a set of Feodor Solntsev's Antiquities of the Russian State, bound in four folio volumes 'presented by His Majesty, the Emperor Alexander II of Russia to the Honorable G.V. Fox, August 1866'; de Pauly's ethnographic description of the peoples of the Russian Empire (including Russian America) – a very highly prized rarity to this day; and several lavishly illustrated presentation volumes depicting the treasures of Tsarskoye Selo, the Winter Palace/Hermitage, and the Patriarchal or Synodal Vestry.

The collection also includes works intended to facilitate the mission, such as a specially-prepared Manual of Russian Conversation and a book of the complex etiquette observed at the Russian court. It is interesting to note the presence of the papers of the Russo-Greek Committee of the Episcopal Church, recording their dialogue with the Orthodox Churches during the nineteenth century.

Not surprisingly, books presented by specifically naval organisations are also found in the collection, including gifts from the Kronstadt Naval Library, the St. Petersburg River Yacht Club (of which Fox was made an honorary member), and issues of the venerable journal Morskoi sbornik. A number of the printed volumes reflect Russo-American economic interests.

Ephemeral materials constitute a particularly intriguing part of the Fox collection as they document Fox's contacts with Russia's political, commercial, and cultural elite. There are letters from provincial mayors, offering to bestow honorary citizenship on Fox. Perhaps the most visually striking of such honorific certificates is a brilliantly illuminated document presented by the city of St. Petersburg. There are many invitations, menus, lists of toasts, specially composed songs and items of correspondence relating to various state functions during Fox's visit, as well as dinners with commercial societies – the Merchants' Club, the Merchants' Assembly, the English Club, and so forth – as well as the speeches made by participants.

Telegrams, toasts, poems, and speeches (both to and by Fox) from the provinces – for example, Lipetsk in south central European Russia, and, far to the east of Moscow, from Tyumen and Ufa, by officials, and even individual peasants and children – are found in abundance among his papers. There are multiple formal invitations to receptions with the Tsar at Peterhof, as well as to military reviews, and dinners hosted by the elite of St. Petersburg society, such as Prince Vasilii Andreevich Dolgorukii (1804-1868), Prince Aleksandr Mikhailovich Gorchakov (1798-1883), Prince Aleksandr Feodorovich Galitzine (Golitsyn, d. 1866), the Grand Duchess Konstantin (d. 1911, wife of Grand Duke Konstantin Nikolaevich (1827-1892), who oversaw the modernisation of Russia's navy after the Crimean War), the Aristocrats' Club, and the 'Noble Birth Society', at the home of Countess Stroganova (1796-1872), in honour of the U.S. Ambassador Cassius M. Clay (d. 1903). There are even original poems: 'Song of Welcome', penned by Oliver Wendell Holmes (1809-1894), to be presented to the Tsar, and 'Greetings to the Atlantic Guest', by Feodor Glinka (1876-1880(?)). There are also cartes de visites, including those of the Empress Maria Aleksandrovna, Alexander III as Tsarevich, Princess Dagmar of Denmark (soon to be Maria Fedorovna II, consort of Alexander III), Grand Duke Konstantin and Grand Duke Alexis.

The cache of Fox materials is especially significant, as the 1860s and 1870s presented America and Russia with an unprecedented opportunity to 'discover' one another's commonalities and differences firsthand. To quote Holmes's poem, read to the Emperor:

Though watery deserts hold apart the worlds of East and West,
Still beats the self-same human heart,
In each proud nation's breast

This article is a version of "The 1866 'Russian Souveniers' of Gustavus Vasa Fox" from the Internatinal Journal Solanus, Vol. 19, 2005

Grand Duke Alexis [right front], at the residence of the Hon. Gustavus V. Fox, Lowell, Massachusetts, December 9, 1871
Photographic print on stereo card
Simon Towle, photographer
Library of Congress

Fox had become acquainted with Grand Duke Alexis during his mission to Russia in 1866 and invited him to his home near Boston when Alexis came to the United States in 1871.

The Russian Pacific Squadron, Navy Yard, Mare Island, California
Unknown artist, ca. 1864
Lithograph
Naval Historical Center

Vessels of the Russian fleet arrived in San Francisco in October 1863. This Pacific Squadron was no less popular than the Atlantic Squadron in New York. During the seven months of the visit of the fleet, five Russian sailors lost their lives helping to put out a massive fire that swept San Francisco.

Lincoln and Slavery

James Oliver Horton

n this age of political "flip-flops", we would do well to remember one of the most important political figures in American history, President Abraham Lincoln, a man who learned from personal experience and changed his mind. In a letter written in 1864, one year before his assassination, Lincoln expressed a view of himself, not for the first time, as one firmly opposed to the institution of slavery. "I am naturally anti-slavery," he wrote. "If slavery is not wrong, nothing is wrong." Then he added an intriguing autobiographical note, "I can not remember when I did not so think, and feel."[1]

By Lincoln's birth in February 1809, African bondage in North America was almost two centuries old. The first Africans were brought to Jamestown, Virginia in 1619 by Dutch traders. These captives worked in the tobacco fields, saving the struggling colony from extinction, helping it to become the first permanent British colony in North America. By the mid-18th century, this informal system of forced labor had become legalized racial slavery, the backbone of European-American agriculture and an important source of workers in all thirteen of the original British colonies.

By the revolutionary period, slavery was firmly rooted in American soil. Slaves heard and understood American claims for natural human rights, listening to the rhetoric of freedom that spurred patriots forward. They challenged their masters to live up to these declarations by abolishing slavery in the emerging nation and sought to expose the hypocrisy of a free nation that tolerated slavery, asking, "Do the rights of nature cease to be such, when a Negro is to enjoy them?"[2] Confronting the American patriots, slaves in Boston added, "We expect great things from men who have made such a noble stand against the designs of the fellow-men to enslave them,"[3]

These protestations were effective in some northern states where slaveholders were less politically powerful than in the South. Throughout New England and in New York, New Jersey, and Pennsylvania, an antislavery spirit pressured government to move against the institution. In these states, constitutions, court rulings, or legislation brought slavery to an end or set it on the road to eventual extinction. There was also strong resistance among many in Congress who believed that slavery should not be allowed to spread into the Northwest territories east of the Mississippi River and north of the Ohio River. Before the adoption of the U.S. Constitution, while the nation was still governed by the Articles of Confederation, Congress passed the Northwest Ordinance of 1787, declaring that "There shall be neither slavery nor involuntary servitude in the said territory, otherwise than in the punishment of crimes whereof the party shall have been duly convicted."[4]

During the early 19th century the free states of Ohio, Indiana, Illinois, Michigan, and Wisconsin were carved from this region. In the South, however, slavery was becoming more entrenched. After invention of the cotton gin in 1793 made cotton processing more efficient and the addition of the Louisiana Territory in 1803 provided the rich fertile soil for the expansion of cotton agriculture, southern slavery grew stronger than ever. By 1815, as cotton textile manufacturing in Europe and in New England expanded, the value of the cotton produced in the new plantation areas of the deep South also rose dramatically, making that region the economic powerhouse of nation. In that year cotton became the single most valuable U.S. export.[5]

Lincoln's home state of Kentucky was originally part of the western region of Virginia and did not share in the slave-fueled prosperity of the deep South. It was more agriculturally diverse than tobacco growing Virginia and grew little cotton. Still, the region's residents held more than 12,000 slaves by 1790. When Kentucky became a state two years later, it retained slavery and the slave population grew substantially. By 1800, there were more than 40,000 slaves in the new state and that number more than doubled by the time of Lincoln's birth.[6] Although there were few large slaveholders in Hardin County where the Lincolns lived, the percentage of slaves there was substantial.[7]

Slaveholding was greatest in the central bluegrass region of the state. There, slaves raised livestock, and grew cereal, other food crops, hemp and tobacco. Some Kentucky slaveholders worked their slaves in salt mines, in iron works, and on bridge and road construction. The presence of slavery was apparently one reason for the Lincoln family's move to Indiana, although it may have been that Thomas was offended as much by the economic competition he faced from slave labor as by the inhumanity of the institution itself. In any case, young Abraham grew to maturity in a free state. However, even people from Free states might expect to encounter slavery on occasion and to confront the unsettling sight of human bondage first-hand. Young Abraham Lincoln had strong memories of his earliest racial encounters in the deep South when he came face to face with the stark inhumanity of slavery. John Hanks, Lincoln's mother's cousin, remembered that he and Lincoln piloted a flatboat to New Orleans, where they saw slaves at auction, "Negroes chained, maltreated, whipped and scourged." Hanks reported that this had a strong effect. "Lincoln saw it, his heart bled, said nothing much, was silent from feeling, was sad, looked bad, felt bad, was thoughtful and abstracted." Hanks was confident, "that it was on this trip that [Lincoln] formed his opinions of slavery; it ran its iron in him then and there."[8]

One sight Lincoln especially remembered and related in many accounts was that of a young mixed-race woman being sold. Prospective buyers handled her as they might a farm animal or an inanimate piece of property. Their close inspection showed no respect for her gender or her humanity. Lincoln was angered by the inhumanity of the entire process, and his emotional response helped shape his lifelong hatred of slavery and of those who profited from it. "If I ever get a chance to hit that thing," he said aloud, "I'll hit it hard."[9]

As the mid-19th century approached, slavery was one of the issues most dangerous to national unity. Americans had already struck a number of compromises in an effort to stave off the massive sectional showdown that some white reformers and many free African Americans were starting to predict. From the beginning, slavery had been too hot to handle, debated but not written into the Constitution except in the most indirect manner. Using euphemistic phrases such as, those not free, or those owing service, the founders insured the constitutional protections of slave property, while not actually calling it by name. As the nation expanded, the growing political and economic power of the slave South forced other compromises, as when the new slave state of Missouri was admitted in the summer of 1821 to balance the free state of Maine admitted a few months before.

The slave South was appeased again in the early 1830s when South Carolina flexed its muscles, opposing the rise in national tariff rates. The federal government seemed to give in to southern concerns by instituting a lower compromise tariff in 1833, demonstrating the South's powerful influence on federal policy. Yet the issue would not rest, surfacing frequently with ever-increasing intensity.

Incensed by the willingness of the federal government to bend to slaveholder demands, some abolitionists called for disunion and violence in support of slaves attempting to escape from bondage. Expressing the sentiments of many in the free black community who feared that the South was exercising intolerable power over federal policy, Frederick Douglass, the abolitionist and former slave, argued that every "slavehunter who meets a bloody death in his infernal business is an argument in favor of the manhood of our [African American] race."[10] Lincoln was not willing to go that far, but he did express his distaste for the bondage that exploited human beings and treated them like a commodity.

The increasingly determined abolitionist attack on slavery was challenged by an equally

Slave collar
Iron, leather
ca. 1840-1865
United States National Slavery Museum

51

aggressive pro-slavery defense. Supporters of slavery rejected the relatively apologetic stance of the old Jeffersonian claim that slavery had been forced on the American colonies by Great Britain's slave traders and was maintained in the new American nation simply as a necessary evil. Jefferson had argued that with tens of thousands of Africans held in bondage within its borders, America was caught in a dangerous quandary. It was, he explained, like "holding a wolf by the ears." The nation could neither hold on nor let go without endangering all that it sought to become.[11]

Lincoln, although not a radical abolitionist, was nevertheless appalled by proslavery claims. He rejected these arguments, responding with characteristic wit. To argue that slavery worked to the advantage of both the slave and the slave master, he observed, was to suppose that the lambs benefited equally with the wolves who devoured them. "Whenever I hear any one arguing for slavery," he remarked "I feel a strong impulse to see it tried on him personally."[12] Beneath this wit however, Lincoln's antislavery position was built on his compassion for those who suffered. He reacted strongly to humanitarian appeals against this evil system that broke up families and destroyed lives for the profit of wealthy and powerful planters in the South, and of northern business interests that financed much of the southern slave system.[13]

By the 1840s, Frederick Douglass, who had escaped from bondage in Maryland in 1838, became one of the most effective antislavery speakers of his generation, telling his personal story of bondage not only in the United States but in Europe as well. A favorite in England and the British Isles, his message that the evil of slavery must be eradicated as a service to Christian principles and to those of America's founding, was one that appealed to Lincoln as

well. Yet both men saw slavery expanding its reach and power in the decades before the Civil War. Cotton grew in national importance as America's single most valuable export, more valuable than all others combined by 1840. Slavery's political power also grew to a formidable force, influencing both southern and national politics, including every presidential election of the period. In 50 of the 72 years between the elections of George Washington and Lincoln, a slaveholder served as president of the United States. Significantly, during those years, only slaveholding presidents were elected to a second term of office.

Lincoln believed that the presence of slavery worked to the disadvantage of many in white society, even as it exploited the labor of blacks to the great advantage of the planter class. While visiting southern Ohio in 1855, he explained to a friend the differences he observed between the characteristics of white people in the slaveholding society in Covington, Kentucky on the south side of the Ohio River, and those in free society in Cincinnati. Although Covington was settled before Cincinnati and had as good a location for trade and commerce, it remained a small town compared to what Lincoln described as "this fine city of Cincinnati." He asked why and then suggested an answer; "just because of slavery, and nothing else." He reasoned that the institution robbed the white population of its ambition and discouraged a respect for industriousness and intellectual pursuit, leaving little incentive for business expansion or economic progress. "That is what slavery does for the white man," he argued. Thus, for Lincoln, the system of slavery posed a hardship for the slave and threatened to retard white society.[14]

Like most white people of his day, Lincoln assumed and accepted white supremacy as a part of the natural order.

However, he was not willing to leave the spread of slavery to the democratic choices of the voting public. Lincoln made an important distinction between his stand on white supremacy and his stand on slavery. "I say upon this occasion, I do not perceive that because the white man is to have the superior position the negro should be denied everything."

Herein lay a thorny problem for the abolitionist movement, for many of their members shared Lincoln's views on race, even as they attacked the racist institution of slavery. Frederick Douglass and other black abolitionists often felt the sting of racial prejudice even from antislavery colleagues. Lincoln was not alone in his racial views among those who opposed slavery. Yet he would change his position during the Civil War as he was presented with evidence that contradicted his early assumptions about race.

During the decades leading to the Civil War it was becoming clear, to those who would see, that slavery was tearing the nation apart. Would America ultimately be the land of the free or the land of the free supported and made prosperous by the toil of slaves? This question became ever more significant as the nation faced the dilemma of its continued expansion. The limitation on the spread of slavery established under the Missouri Compromise of 1820 was challenged when Congress adopted the Kansas-Nebraska bill in 1854 that opened areas north of the Missouri's southern boundary to the institution if those settling in that region desired it. Under this proposition there might be no predetermined limits to the spread of slavery. Lincoln could imagine no "more apt invention to bring about collision and violence on the slavery question."[15]

He was right to worry. The settlement of Kansas brought the country to the brink of war as the forces of antislavery and proslavery clashed over the future of the territory. Lincoln attempted to calm his colleagues in the Whig Party, urging against violence in Kansas. "Physical rebellion and bloody resistance," he argued, "were not only wrong, but also unconstitutional."[16]

During the mid-1850s Lincoln played a leading role in the construction of the new Republican Party that united the anti-slavery movement. Clearly, in the decade before the Civil War, slavery had become the central point of contention dividing the nation, threatening to sever the slaveholding South from the free-labor North. Lincoln stood in a precarious middle ground, not demanding the abolition of slavery in the South, but determined to limit its expansion. While he did not favor an abolitionist for the top of the Republic presidential ticket in 1856, he did believe that the party and its candidate must take a stand on slavery. He was infuriated by the violence in Kansas and by the attack on Massachusetts Senator Charles Sumner by South Carolina Representative Preston Brooks, who had taken exception to Sumner's antislavery position and his verbal attack on a South Carolina senator. After hearing the news of Brooks' beating of Sumner on the floor of the Senate, Lincoln, who saw this as yet another proslavery aggression, reportedly "stepped cleanly out of his character and became . . . a different person–fiery, emotional, reckless, violent, hot blooded–everything which at other times he was not."[17]

Lincoln's anger and reported loss of self-control mirrored the reaction of many Americans to the growing national confrontation over slavery. When he ran for the presidency as the Republican candidate in 1860, he did so not as an abolitionist but as one committed to con-

taining what he had grown to see as a cancerous institution. When he won election, he attempted to reassure the slave states that had declared their separation from the nation and those that had remained loyal, that he had no intention of interfering with slavery in the states where it currently existed. Despite his earlier antislavery statements, his main concern, Lincoln told the nation, was to hold the union together and he would do that with or without slavery. In an 1862 letter to newspaper editor Horace Greeley, he explained his position in detail, "My paramount object in this struggle is to save the Union, and is not either to save or to destroy slavery. If I could save the Union without freeing any slave I would do it, and if I could save it by freeing all the slaves I would do it; and if I could save it by freeing some and leaving others alone I would also do that. What I do about slavery, and the colored race, I do because I believe it helps to save the Union."[18]

Slavery deeply affected Lincoln's presidency as it had affected much of his life and the life of the nation. It drove the movement for southern secession and shaped his efforts to save the nation.

After the confederates fired on Fort Sumter on April 12, 1861, Lincoln issued a call for seventy-five thousand volunteers to protect the Union. Within days, another four states,

John Wilkes Booth
Albumen print on Carte de Visite
Silsbee, Case and Company of Boston, ca. 1860
Erie County Historical Society, Erie, PA

Emancipation Proclamation
Lithograph
B.B. Russell & Co., Boston, 1865
Lincoln College Museum, Lincoln, Illinois

Virginia, Arkansas, Tennessee and North Carolina, withdrew from the Union. Slavery was the central issue – its defense motivated southern secession, and secession moved Lincoln and the North to save the country from disaster.

By the fall of 1862, Lincoln turned to the abolition of slavery and the recruitment of African American soldiers as a means of winning the

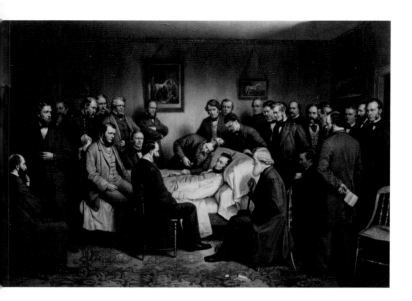

Death of Lincoln
Mezzotint
Alexander Hay Ritchie; A.H. Ritchie, New York, 1868
McLellan Lincoln Collection, John Hay Library, Brown University

war against the slave power. Although his Emancipation Proclamation that took effect January 1, 1863 only applied to slaves then under the control of Confederate forces, it was a critical step towards ending the slave system. After Lincoln's proclamation, the tens of thousands of slaves who escaped the Confederacy and flocked U.S. lines found freedom immediately.

The more than 200,000 blacks who served in the union military during the war were instrumental in the U.S. victory and impressed Lincoln greatly.

Despite his earlier belief that African Americans were unfit for the rights and privileges of full citizenship, by 1865 Lincoln called not only for black freedom but also for a measure of political equality. His murderer, John

Wilkes Booth, found Lincoln's support for the idea that black soldiers and educated blacks should be allowed full voting rights intolerable. By the end of his life, Lincoln had set slavery on the road to extinction by his proclamation and his advocacy of the 13th Amendment to the U.S. Constitution. He was killed for his willingness to end slavery and to move beyond freedom towards racial equality.

Lincoln did not live to see slavery's demise, yet for generations after his assassination Abraham Lincoln has remained to Americans of all races, the man who ended slavery, the Great Emancipator.

Mourning Badge
Celluloid, wigan, satin, wire
1865
National Park Service, Ford's Theatre National Historic Site

Lincoln Memorial, Washington, D.C.
Photo by Reid Buckley

Footnotes

[1] This article is a version of Dr. Horton's "Naturally Anti-Slavery: Lincoln, Race, and the Complexity of American Liberty" from *Lincoln Lore: The Bulletin of the Lincoln Museum,* No. 1890, Fall, 2007, pp. 18-27. A. Lincoln to Albert G. Hodges, April 4, 1864," Michael P. Johnson, ed., Abraham Lincoln, Slavery, and the Civil War: Selected Writings and Speeches, (Boston: St Martin's Bedford Books, 2000), 285.

[2] Philip Foner, *History of Black Americans: From Africa to the Emergence of the Cotton Kingdom,* I (Westport, CN: Greenwood Press, 1975), 297.

[3] Circular letter Boston, April 20, 1773 (The New York Historical Society).

[4] Theodore C. Pease, "The Ordinance of 1787," Miss. Valley Historical .Review, 25 (1938): 167-180; Christine Compston and Rachel Filene Seidman, eds. Our Documents: 100 Milestone Documents from the National Archives. (New York: Oxford University Press, 2003), 27.

[5] The Cotton Gin, invented by Eli Whitney made it possible for a slave to process fifty pounds of cotton per day, removing cotton seeds from the fiber, an increase of fifty fold. It received a patent on March 14, 1794. See Angela Lakwete, Inventing the Cotton Gin: Machine and Myth in Antebellum America (Baltimore: John Hopkins University Press, 2003).

[6] Negro Population in the United States, 1790-1915 (New York: Arno Press and the New York Times, 1968), 57.

[7] Paul Simon, Lincoln's Preparation for Greatness: The Illinois Legislative Years (Urbana: University of Illinois Press, 1971), 128.

[8] Douglas L. Wilson and Rodney O. Davis, eds. Herndon's Informants : Letters, Interviews, and Statements about Abraham Lincoln (Urbana : University of Illinois Press, 1997), 457. Allen Guelzo finds Hank's account suspect and argues that Hanks never completed the trip to New Orleans and may have confused this trip with an earlier one in 1828. See Allen C. Guelso, Abraham Lincoln: Redeemer President (Grand Rapids, MI: Wm. B. Eerdmans Publishing, 1999), 128.

[9] Benjamin Quarles, Lincoln and the Negro (New York: Oxford University Press, 1962), 18.

[10] James Oliver Horton and Lois E. Horton, Black Bostonians: Family Life and Community Struggle in the Antebellum North (New York: Holmes and Meier Publishers, 1979, Second edition, 1999), 111-113.

[11] John Chester Miller, Wolf by the Ears: Thomas Jefferson and Slavery (New York: Free Press, 1977).

[12] Burlingame, 33; "Speech to One Hundred Fortieth Indiana Regiment, March 17, 1865" in Roy P. Basler, ed., The Collected Works of Abraham Lincoln, (New Brunswick, NJ : Rutgers University Press, 1953), 361.

[13] Anne Farrow, Joel Lang, and Jenifer Frank Complicity: How the North Promoted, Prolonged, and Profited from Slavery (New York: Ballantine Books, 2005).

[14] Burlingame, 30.

[15] David Donald, Lincoln (New York: Simon & Schuser, 1995),188.

[16] Ibid.

[17] Burlingame, 159.

[18] "Letter to Horace Greeley" (August 22, 1862), Basler, Volume 5, p. 388.

A Royal Visit:
The Grand Duke Alexis in the United States

Suzanne Massie

n the 19th century gestures of friendship between Imperial Russia and our young republic abounded and the United States considered Russia to be one of its firmest supporters in the international community. These friendly relations reached a peak in the 1860s and '70s during the reign of Tsar Alexander II. Because of his many social economic and political reforms and his crowning achievement, the liberation of the serfs in 1861, the emperor was an object of respect and even veneration in the United States.

In 1860, Alexander II wrote admiringly of the United States. When the French urged the English and the Russians toward full recognition of the Confederacy, the Imperial Government refused and in 1863 at a critical moment in the Civil War a Russian steam frigate and two Russian corvettes steamed into New York harbor, followed by the news that another Russian fleet had arrived in San Francisco. Jubilation reigned all over America. Lincoln referred to the Russian visits in his Thanksgiving Proclamation as "God's bounties of so extraordinary a nature that they cannot fail to penetrate the heart."

It was in the glow of these good feelings that Russian-American negotiations for the sale of Alaska were completed in 1867. The Alaska purchase was a solid achievement, but for the general public it lacked bright colors and a human figure on which to focus. In contrast, the high point of Russian-American friendship was the good will visit in 1871-72 by the Grand Duke Alexis, the third son of the Tsar Liberator. The United States had had only one previous royal visitor in its history—the visit in 1860 of the Prince of Wales who was officially incognito. The Grand Duke Alexis was our first and only

The Royal Buffalo Hunt
Joe Grandee, ca.1971
Oil on canvas
Private collection

Riding in the buffalo hunt, General Custer is seen at the far left; Grand Duke Alexis is in the center, forefront; Buffalo Bill Cody is just to the left, behind the Grand Duke. General Sheridan is seen on the right, with pistol poised.

imperial visitor, an authentic Romanov who came from faraway Russia trailing the glamour of the tsars. The excitement of the American people and press boiled over.

The Grand Duke Alexis arrived in New York on November 20, 1871 and left on February 23, 1872. In those three months he visited 34 American cities, was seen by most of the popu-

lation of America, hunted on the prairies, and made so pronounced an imprint on the Mardi Gras in New Orleans that he is still remembered and enshrined in that city. All over the land he was wined, dined, pampered, ogled, and adored by most of the feminine population of America. At the time Alexis was 21 years old, a lieutenant in the Imperial Navy, well over six feet tall, blonde, husky with tidily clipped mutton chop whiskers and pensive blue eyes. Like other members of the Russian aristocracy he spoke several languages including fluent but accented English. He speeches were always gracious and to the point. He was a sportsman, good at wrestling, hunting, and riding–a jolly fellow who enjoyed fine cigars and wine, loved opera and musical comedies, and delighted in singing in his fine bass voice. Although not a very good dancer, he exhibited extraordinary stamina on the dance floor, surviving a marathon of balls and leading a small army of cooing ladies out into quadrilles, waltzes and gallops.

The Grand Duke's official visit lasted six weeks packed with official receptions, balls, parades, reviews, toasts and testimonials to Russia "our most steadfast and unswerving friend" from governors, senators, congressmen, mayors, and presidents of universities. America was seized with Grand Dukeomania. Alexis led a special parade up Broadway festooned with American and Russian flags, visited West Point, and inspected America's latest torpedoes and coastal artillery at the Brooklyn Navy Yard. He went on to Philadelphia and then Washington where he was received at the White House by President Grant and met the famous war hero and Indian fighter Phil Sheridan, to whom he expressed a keen interest in the wonders of the American West and his dream of hunting buffalo. Alexis continued on to Connecticut and Massachusetts, spending a week in Boston greeted by cheering crowds in Harvard Square, a sumptuous grand ball in the Boston Theater, and a gala banquet at Revere House attended by 200 distinguished gentlemen including Oliver Wendell Holmes, Henry Wadsworth Longfellow, James Russell Lowell, the Mayor of Boston, and the Governor of Massachusetts. Then he was off to Canada, Niagara Falls, and Buffalo where more than 20,000 people including former President Millard Fillmore waited in the snow on Christmas Eve to greet him. Next was Cleveland, Detroit, and Chicago where he inspected the devastating effects of the Chicago fire and left the Mayor a donation of $5,000 in gold to distribute among the victims. After stopping in Milwaukee and then in St Louis, his official tour ended.

But the best was yet to come. In the weeks that followed, the Grand Duke was to live some of the adventures of which Russian boys dreamed, savoring the excitement of the Wild West, hunting on the prairies with Buffalo Bill Cody, General George Custer, the U.S. Cavalry, and a troop of Sioux Indians. Ending his trip with a flourish, he went down the Mississippi with George and Libby Custer to the Mardi Gras in New Orleans where the inhabitants prepared a special welcome for him.

While Alexis was occupied touring the Midwest, General Phil Sheridan had been busy. Before Alexis had left the White House, President Grant had instructed that the War Department's entire Western Division be at his disposal and Sheridan had personally offered to organize a buffalo hunt in the Republican River region of Nebraska where the General had fought several Indian battles in 1868-69. As a national war hero with the backing of the President, Sheridan was in a position to organize in grand style the hunt he had promised.

The Grand Duke's party traveled from St. Louis to North Platte in a special five car train of new Pullman cars sumptuously outfitted. Sheridan had hired Buffalo Bill Cody, the most famous citizen of North Platte to come along. At 25, the flamboyant scout and Pony Express rider already had a national reputation for his adventures on the prairies and was considered the finest buffalo hunter in the West. To provide authentic local color, Sheridan asked Bill to find the famous Sioux Chief Spotted Tail and hire him plus an entourage of a thousand Indians, male and female. Cody closed the deal by promising Spotted Tail 1,000 pounds of tobacco.

To receive the Grand Duke, the U.S. Army worked feverishly to set up a proper camp–Camp Alexis–in the middle of buffalo country, clearing four acres of snow in mid-winter. Privies were dug, flagpoles raised, mountains of firewood cut, and bonfires laid. Two huge hospital tents and many wall tents were pitched for the Grand Duke, the generals, and their friends, plus 40 more tents for attendants, military escorts, orderlies, and servants. New bedding, carpets, tables and chairs arrived from Chicago. The Grand Duke arrived in Omaha on January 12 where thousands had gathered to greet him. Waiting at the station were Sheridan, two other generals, and a Citizen Committee of dignitaries as well as 32 year-old George Custer who had been summoned from Kentucky to be Grand Marshal of the four day hunt. After a rollicking 15 hour train trip across the prairie, they arrived in North Platte where Buffalo Bill, mounted on a splendid horse, was waiting. Over six feet tall, he cut an impressive figure in his spangled buckskin suit, coat trimmed with fur, and black slouch hat. The whole town watched as a caravan of over 500 people formed–ambulance wagons, baggage wagons, two companies of infantry, two cavalry companies, a regimental band, outriders and cooks, three wagons of champagne and spirits, some Indians, and two enterprising reporters As they traveled, the American officers entertained their Russian visitors with tales and reminiscences of their life and adventure on the plains. Eight hours later, upon reaching Camp Alexis, the band broke into the Russian national anthem, followed by an excellent meal of differ-ent varieties of game found on the Western prairies washed down with choice wines.

January 14 was the Grand Duke's 22 birthday. Buffalo Bill returned from his early scouting announcing a large herd of buffalo thirteen miles away. After a breakfast washed down with champagne toasts, they galloped off, followed by reporters and the rest of the company. Buffalo Bill led them around ravines for thirteen miles until they sighted the large herd. The Grand Duke missed his first shots, but Cody, handing him his Springfield rifle, urged him on, and the Grand Duke brought down a big bull. He whooped with joy and servants galloped up with baskets of champagne, a bottle for each hunter. They rode back to the camp at sunset, announcing their arrival with wild Indian yells, which were answered by Spotted Tail and his braves. The next day Sheridan, the Grand Duke, Buffalo Bill, and Custer, accompanied by Spotted Tail, other famous chiefs and their bands of Sioux braves, set out–the Indians armed only with bows and arrows. They rode so well and shot so brilliantly that the Grand Duke was awestruck. That night the Indians held a War Dance in his honor, dancing and chanting their exploits while an interpreter stood beside the Grand Duke to translate. The Grand Duke presented gifts to Spotted Tail's tribe and invited the chief, his wife, and daughter, a maiden of 16, to the dining tent for champagne and food. After dinner, the young maiden gathered all the fragments of the dinner and tucked them into her blanket. The evening finished with a ceremonial smoking of the peace pipe.

Custer and the Grand Duke had become such good friends as they galloped over the prairies that Custer asked Sheridan for permission to accompany Alexis for the rest of his stay in America. Sheridan agreed and Custer invited Alexis to visit Kentucky and then to steam

Grand Duke Alexis (rt) and General George Custer on their trip across the prairies
Reproduced from the Collections of the Library of Congress

down the Mississippi to the Mardi Gras in New Orleans. Traveling by train from North Platte, they whistle-stopped through small western towns where even in the dead of night crowds turned out. In Cheyenne the whole town came to serenade them. After 19 hours they reached Denver to find several thousands more waiting for them in the snow. More buffalo hunting followed in Colorado, a whirlwind tour through Louisville and Memphis, and then on to the Mardi Gras.

To make the four day trip from Memphis to New Orleans, the Grand Duke chartered the 320 foot James Howard, known as "Oil Cake Jim," the largest side-wheeler on the Mississippi. Joining him and his suite of nine were General and Mrs. Custer, two Louisville belles, and from Memphis a Mr. Vance and his two daughters. The Grand Duke was informed of the towns they passed and the length of rivers by his English tutor, but clearly preferred the company of the girls, music, and singing.

In New Orleans when they had first heard the news that the Grand Duke was to come, the detested carpetbagger city government made no special plans to greet him. But two weeks before his scheduled arrival a group of New Orleans gentlemen, deciding that the hospitality of their city was at stake, dreamed up a plan. Why not form the previous motley and disorganized masquers, who at the time randomly roamed the street at Mardi Gras, into a proper procession that would honor the Grand Duke? Why not create a royal personage–a king–who would rule over the proceedings and be able to welcome the Grand Duke on an equal footing? Thus was created Mardi Gras as it is celebrated today. Within 24 hours they had gathered a group of 30 members (later 40). One of the original group, banker Lewis Salomon, was delegated to raise the $5,000 necessary to mount their plan. He was so successful, promising every contributor of $100 to make him a duke, that he was named Rex–although his identity was kept a closely guarded secret. At first the city government was horrified, but after enlisting the permission of the mayor and the police chief, the mysterious Rex plunged ahead. Comically pompous edicts and proclamations from the new king were published daily in the newspapers, and the delighted city happily joined in the proceedings. Rex ordered the masquers to organize to "do him honor," the artillery to turn out, and all businesses and banks to close and give their employees the day off. All inhabitants were to decorate their houses with his official colors of purple, green, and gold; all bands were commanded to play his official anthem.

The organizing group secretly borrowed royal costumes from a theater where a noted actor was playing Richard III. Workmen erected an elaborate reviewing stand festooned with the red, white, and blue Imperial flag along with a great arch of gas jets with crystal shades of many colors for night viewing. Under a canopy of crimson silk fringed with gold festoons stood an imperial throne for Alexis. Flocks of visitors began streaming into the city. On February 12, the Grand Duke steamed down to the levee at Gravier Street Wharf. Steamboat whistles shrilled, flags waved, and people on other riverboats hung over their railings cheering.

It was delightedly whispered about the city that there were other inducements that had attracted the Grand Duke to the romantic city of New Orleans besides filigreed porches. Two of the most popular musical comedy stars of American stage were appearing simultaneously in the city during carnival. One was Lydia Thompson, and her troop of British Blondes, whom the Grand Duke had first seen in New York in her smash hit, "The Burlesque of Bluebeard," and highly appreciated her songs, especially "If Ever I Cease to Love." The other was the petite, vivacious Lotta Mignon Crabtree who at 24 was the most popular star in America, so famous that she was known simply as "Little Lotta" and had two baseball teams named after her. In February 1872 she was appearing at the St. Charles, the finest theater in the country, which seated over 4,000 people. Hardly had Alexis arrived before he expressed the desire to meet the lovely Lotta, and invited her to a sumptuous ten course dinner at the St Charles Hotel where she was seated between the Grand Duke and Custer.

On February 13, the day of Mardi Gras, every house and place of business was covered with wide bands of purple, gold, and green. A popular tradition was begun that day, for these symbols and emblems have remained the permanent symbol of Carnival. The first formal Mardi Gras parade followed–15,000 people all in costume. The two distinguished royal personages, Rex and the Grand Duke, met on the

Box of Grand Duke Alexis Alexandrovich
St. Petersburg, 1880-1890 Firm of Faberge, workmaster:
J. Rappoport Silver, engraving, gilding
State Historical Museum, Moscow

The box is set with eight engraved images of Russian naval vessels under the command of Grand Duke Alexis when he became Admiral of the Russian Navy. His crowned cypher appears at center on the top of the box.

reviewing stand. The bands played the "official" anthem of Rex which turned out to be the best joke of the day—Lydia Thompson's hit song "If Ever I Cease to Love"—and won such a cherished place in the heart of New Orleans that it is still the theme song of Mardi Gras. The Grand Duke had such a good time in New Orleans that he postponed his departure from day to day. He attended Lotta's performance on Valentine's Day and, before he left, presented her with an elegant jeweled bracelet. Finally, on February 19 the Grand Duke boarded his special train to rejoin the Russian fleet at Pensacola, warmly embracing his friend Custer and saluting the crowd of 2,000 who waved their handkerchiefs in farewell.

Although they were never to meet again, Alexis and Custer regularly exchanged letters

until Custer's death at Little Big Horn. Alexis in later years became Admiral of the Russian Navy, but his visit and his days galloping over the prairies with his friend Custer were the most carefree and joyous of his life. The world of Buffalo Bill and Custer, Lydia and Lotta is gone now. The Romanovs have been swept

Portrait of Grand Duke Nicholas Alexandrovich in the winter jacket of the Grodno Hussar Life Guards
Georg Bothman, 1868
Oil on canvas
State Museum-Preserve "Tsarskoye Selo"

The eldest son of Alexander II died of a rare form of tubercular meningitis in Nice at the age of twenty-one. Known as 'Niks' to his family and friends, he was, by all accounts, a charming and remarkable young man. He bore the last weeks of his painful, undiagnosed illness with such courage and piety that everyone around him was greatly moved. His parents were at his bedside when he died on April 24, 1865. Helped by his sons, the Emperor himself prepared the body and laid it to rest in the coffin. The personal lives of Alexander II and Marie Alexandrovna were forever changed by this tragic loss.

This portrait was commissioned after the death of Niks and hung in the study of Alexander II.

Photograph of Alexander II with his family
Unknown photographer, late 1860s
Mounted photograph
State Archive of the Russian Federation

This photograph was taken several years after the tragic death of the Tsar's eldest son and heir, Nicholas Alexandrovich, in Nice in 1865. There is a look of sadness in the expression of Empress Marie Alexandrovna, seated center, who never recovered from the death of her favorite son.

Surrounding the Imperial couple are their remaining six children, from left to right: Grand Duchess Marie, Grand Duke Sergei, Grand Duke Alexis (standing), Grand Duke Paul, Grand Duke and succeeding Tsarevich, Alexander with his wife, Tsarevna Marie Feodorovna (the future parents of Nicholas II), and Grand Duke Vladimir (standing to the right of Alexander II, seated).

away, but in New Orleans, the Grand Duke permanently captured the imagination of the people. After his visit, Mardi Gras was declared an official state holiday. The dynasty of Rex endures. Every year in New Orleans the purple green and gold flags wave and "If Ever I Cease to Love" rings joyously in the streets, the lasting legacy of what was certainly the coziest and most intimate chapter in the history of Russian-American relations.

The Final Years
of the Tsar-Liberator

Ludmila Kanaeva

"So this is what we have come to!"
Grand Duke Alexander Alexandrovich
at the bedside of the dying Alexander II.

he final years of Alexander II's reign were not easy for him. By the end of the 1870s the transformations he had brought about should already have produced results. In reality, however, everything was much more complicated. The reforms carried out at the emperor's initiative, which had demanded great effort and also some courage, were not proceeding as smoothly as had been expected, and Alexander's countrymen were far from unanimous in accepting them. He shared the fate of all reformers - the unjust judgment of his contemporaries. In all the reforms Alexander II undertook, he was criticized from both the right and left. Some thought the reforms too revolutionary, others thought them insufficient and half-hearted.

"On the day the serfs were freed, Alexander II was adored in Petersburg," writes one memoirist. Nonetheless, almost immediately after publication of the decree abolishing serfdom, proclamations began to circulate in Petersburg in which radicals called for popular revolt and violence against the emperor. Several copies of these proclamations turned up even in the Winter Palace. Petr Valuev, minister of the interior, mentions several times in his diary that such appeals were circulating in the capital. In May of 1862 he wrote: "A new production of the Young Russia press is being spread around the city. It openly calls for regicide, for the murder of the entire imperial house and all their supporters, proclaiming the most extreme socialist principles, and foretelling a 'Russian red, socialist republic.'"

Russian peasants thanking Alexander II for their liberation from serfdom
Chromolithograph after the original by B. Rozhansky
A.Belozerov publication, 1860s
State Historical Museum, Moscow

Alexander II is seen in an open carriage leaving the Winter Palace with peasants gathered around him expressing their gratitude.

This social tension eventually led to active terrorism by revolutionary extremists. Their main target was the emperor, whom they saw at the embodiment of tyranny and despotism. We know of several attempts on Alexander II's life. The first of these was on April 4, 1866. Dmitri Karakozov fired a shot at Alexander in the Summer Garden, where he was accustomed to go for walks. The bullet missed only because of the peasant Komisarov, a former serf, who struck the terrorist's arm as he was firing.

Portrait of Alexander II wearing the uniform of a general
Oil on canvas
Pavel Antonov, 1875
State Museum-Preserve "Tsarskoye Selo"

Painted just six years before the tsar's assassination, this portrait reveals a "change" in his facial expression.

Attempt on the life of Alexander II. Explosion of the second bomb, March 1, 1881
Lithograph, from the original by A. Baldniger
Moscow, 1881
State Historical Museum, Moscow

On May 25, 1867, there was a second assassination attempt, in Paris, by A. Berezovsky. The emperor was greatly affected and took a long time to recover his usual spirits. More than a month after the attempt, he told one of his entourage: "I do not know what has happened to me, but I have never been the way I am now, and I feel changed. Nothing gives me any pleasure."

In the late 1870s the revolutionary movement broadened in Russia, and the government reacted with repressions. In turn the most implacable revolutionaries, the terrorists, condemned Alexander to death and proclaimed a "hunt" for him. "This magnanimous monarch, who had done great deeds and deserved boundless gratitude from all Russian people, was hounded like a wild beast," wrote one of the public figures of that time. Even on April 17, 1878–his 60th birthday–there was no rest for Alexander. Instead, he held an urgent meeting with his ministers "on adopting decisive measures to put down revolutionary schemes, which are becoming ever more audacious." At the conference the

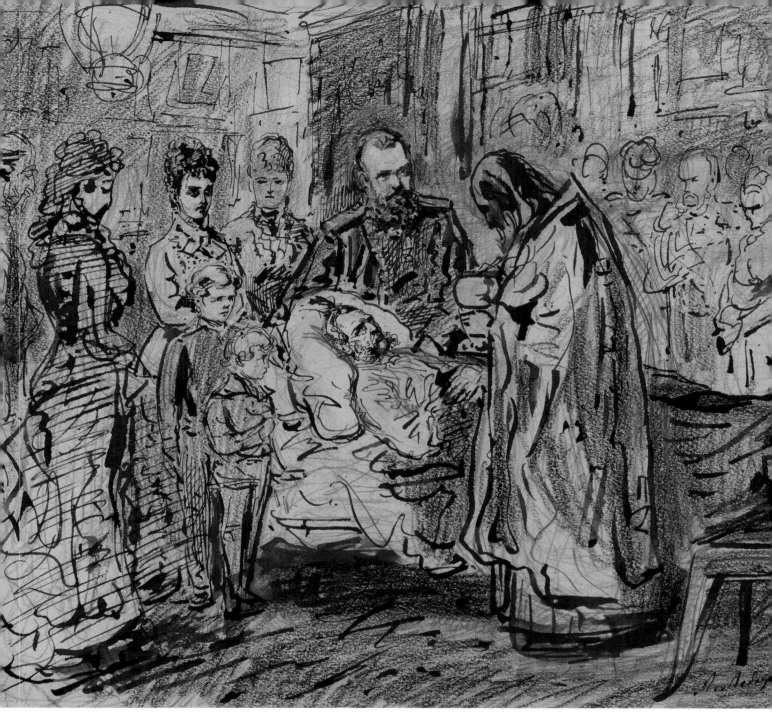

Last Minutes in the Life of Emperor Alexander II
Pencil drawing
A.Lebedev, 1881
State Historical Museum, Moscow

The family is gathered around the deathbed in the tsar's study in the Winter Palace. The tsarevich, Grand Duke Alexander Alexandrovich, who will become Alexander III, stands over his father conversing with a priest in attendance, standing to the right. Two little grandsons, Nicholas (the future Nicholas II) and his younger brother, George, stand to the left of the bed.

gloomy, troubled tsar remarked, "And this is how I have to spend my birthday!"

Alexander survived two assassination attempts in 1879. Alexander Solovyev shot at him on April 2, in Palace Square. In November, members of the group, The People's Will, blew up a section of railroad line outside Moscow, where the emperor's train was scheduled to travel. The train arrived half an hour early, and catastrophe was avoided.

On February 5, 1880, another member of The People's Will, Stepan Khalturin, organized a bombing in the Winter Palace. The explosion took place in the guard post below the dining room, at a time when Alexander was supposed to have been there with his family. Luckily, dinner on that day had been set for a later time than usual because a guest was expected. But more than forty soldiers of the Finnish Regiment's Life Guards were killed or hurt. The explosion was so powerful that it was heard in houses on the Moyka embankment. Count Dmitri Milyutin, who was in the palace that day, remarked in his diary that Alexander had been remarkably self-possessed, and added a thought that occurred to many in the tsar's entourage. He wrote: "This incident is particularly shocking. Anyone must ask where peace and safety can be found, if the evildoers can lay mines in the tsar's palace itself." The following day a large public event was held as planned at the Winter Palace. The sovereign was "very distraught, but appeared calm, said a few words, which he could not finish without tears, said that he hoped the people would help him to crush sedition, that the Lord had saved him yet again, that he relied on us all, that evil must be rooted out."

Despite all protective measures, another attempt on Alexander's life took place on March 1, 1881. This time the outcome was fatal. Afterwards the day was reconstructed hour by hour. In the morning the tsar went from the Winter Palace to the Mikhailov riding school to see the mounting of the guard. Afterwards he went to see Grand Duchess Ekaterina Mikhailovna at the Mikhailov Palace. Bomb-throwers lay in wait along the road back, on the embankment of the Catherine canal." The sovereign came out of the above-mentioned palace at 2:10, and seating himself in the carriage said to the coachman, 'Home by the same way,'" wrote A. Dvorzhitsky, a chief of police who traveled with the emperor on his last journey and was an eye witness to all these events. "After riding down Engineer Street and turning towards the Catherine Canal, His Majesty greeted the guards of the 8th Fleet company, who were returning from their watch. The coachman turned the horses full speed down the embankment, but before they had gone a hundred sazhens [about 210 meters] there was a deafening blast, which did severe damage to the sovereign's carriage. Two Cossacks in the escort were injured, along with a peasant boy and my horses." It was Nikolai Rysakov who threw the bomb under the emperor's carriage as it passed. The carriage stopped. "I ran at once to the sovereign's carriage, helped him out, and reported that the criminal had been detained. The sovereign was completely calm. To my question about his well-being he answered, 'Thank God, I am not wounded.' Seeing that the carriage was damaged, I allowed myself to offer His Highness my own sleigh for the return to the palace. To this he answered, 'Good, but first show me the criminal.' First Alexander went up to Rysakov, then asked to have a look at the place where the explosion had been. At that moment a man standing at the canal railing threw a bomb between Alexander and himself. This was Ignati Grinevitsky, another member of The People's Will. The explosion mortally wounded both

"The demise of His Imperial Majesty, the Sovereign Emperor Alexander II. Catafalque in the palace church"
Popular print of a lithograph
V.V. Ponomaryov, Moscow, 1881
State Archive of the Russian Federation, Moscow

Alexander and his assassin. "Suddenly, amid the smoke and the snowy mist," Dvorzhitsky remembered, "I heard the faint voice of His Highness: 'Help!' … His Majesty was half-sitting, half-lying, resting on his right elbow. Supposing that he was severely wounded but no more, I lifted him a little off the ground, and saw with horror that both his legs were blown to bits and streaming blood." The wounded emperor was put into a sleigh and taken to the Winter Palace. He was carried into his study. The court doctor on duty was called to help the dying emperor. He later recalled those minutes: "When I rushed up to the bed, what struck my eye immediately were the horribly disfigured lower limbs, especially the left, which was a formless, shattered, bloody mass from the knee to the half torn-off foot. The right limb

was also wounded, but less. The right boot was still on its foot, the left was gone."

The tsar was unconscious. The tsarevich asked how long his father had left, and Botkin, the physician in ordinary, said ten or fifteen minutes. "Then the tsarevich turned away from his dying father's bed and cried bitterly, saying 'So this is what we have come to!' and then fervently embraced Grand Dukes Vladimir Alexandrovich and Mikhail Nicholaevich." Alexander II died at three-thirty in the afternoon without having regained consciousness.

Life's last minutes had run out for Alexander II, the Tsar-Liberator, and "one of the greatest reigns in Russian history ended in a bloody drama unheard of in our chronicles."

St. Petersburg. Church of the Resurrection of Christ
(Saviour on the Blood) built on the site of the lethal wounding of Alexander II
Color autotype, ca 1910
State Historical Museum, Moscow

This surviving monument dedicated to Alexander II was begun in 1883 and completed in 1907. Popularly known as the Church of the Saviour on the Blood, it was built in accordance with the ancient tradition of memorial churches in Russia, and intended for special services in memory of Alexander II. In recent years, it has been re-opened as a museum following a long period of restoration.

Excerpts From Historic Letters and Dispatches

1. The position of Russia with regard to the Civil War in the United States is expressed in this official communication of Prince Gorchakov to Edouard de Stoeckl, Russian Envoy in Washington, sent eleven days before the first battle of Bull Run:

Dispatch of Minister of Foreign Affairs of the Russian Empire, A.M. Gorchakov, to the Russian Envoy in the United States, E.A. Stoeckl June 28/July 10, 1861

"...for the more than eighty years that it has existed the American Union owes its independence, its towering rise, and its progress, to the concord of its members, consecrated, under the auspices of its illustrious founder, by institutions which have been able to reconcile union with liberty. It would be deplorable that, after so conclusive an experience, the United States should be hurried into a breach of the solemn pact which, up to his time, made their power.... In our view, this Union is not only a substantial element of the world political equilibrium, but additionally, it represents the nation towards which our Sovereign and Russia as a whole, display the friendliest interest, since the two countries located at the ends of two worlds, during the previous period of their development seemed to have been called to a natural solidarity of interests and leanings which they have already proven to each other. . . . In all cases, the American Union may count on the most heart-felt sympathy on the part of the Sovereign in the course of the serious crisis which the Union is currently going through."

Added notation of Alexander II: "So be it"

Archive of the Foreign Ministry of the Russian Empire, in French

2. The Great Reforms of Alexander II in 1861-62 included a Judicial Reform decreed on September 29, 1862. It greatly impressed the U.S. Charge d'Affaires in St. Petersburg, Bayard Taylor, who sent a lengthy report to the Secretary of State.

Dispatch of the U.S. Charge d' Affaires in St. Petersburg, Bayard Taylor, to Secretary of State William H. Seward on the Judicial Reform issued by Alexander II
October 25, 1862

> *"Sir: I have the honor to report to you the promulgation of a decree of his Imperial Majesty which is universally pronounced to be second in importance in its effect upon the future of Russia only to that of the emancipation of the serfs.* It is no less than a plan or basis for the thorough reorganization of the administration of justice throughout the empire, whereby the innumerable abuses, possibly under the prevailing system, are prevented, and the great body of the people receive, in addition to personal liberty, an equal protection in the enjoyment of their individual rights.....*

U. S. National Archives and Records Administration

3. In his response, Secretary of State Seward expressed the friendship of the United States toward Russia:

Dispatch of Secretary of State William H. Seward to Bayard Taylor, U.S. Charge d' Affairs
November 24, 1862

> *"The decree of the Emperor which establishes an independent and impartial judiciary...is calculated to command the approval of mankind. It seems to secure to Russia the benefits without the calamities of revolution...Constitutional nations which heretofore have regarded the friendship between Russia and the United States as wanting a foundation in common principles and sentiments, must hereafter admit that this relation is as natural in its character as it is auspicious to both countries in its result....*

U.S. National Archives and Records Administration

4. The enthusiastic welcome given to the sailors from the Russian naval squadron in New York in September 1863 was reported to Prince Gorchakov by Edouard de Stoeckl. This response expresses the personal gratitude of Alexander II to President Lincoln.

Dispatch of the Minister of Foreign Affairs A.M. Gorchakov to Russian Envoy in the United States E.A. Stoeckl
November 14, 1863

The Foreign Minister reports to Stoeckl that he has passed the report about the heart-felt welcome given to the sailors from Admiral Lissovki's naval squadron in New York to Alexander II. He relates the Emperor's order to express gratitude to President Lincoln, emphasizing that such "evidence of gratitude and good will are the best proof of friendly relations that unite both countries. They can only contribute to the strengthening of such relations, since the Russian people value very highly the welcoming of the courageous sailors who had been entrusted with the honor of the national flag in this far-away land."

Note of Alexander II: "So be it"

Archive of the Foreign Ministry of the Russian Empire

5. This letter of Alexander II to President Andrew Johnson is his response on receiving the Congressional Resolution expressing the nation's gratitude for the Tsar's escape from an assassin's attempt on his life. The Resolution was delivered personally to the Tsar by Gustavus V. Fox on his naval mission to Russia in 1866.

Letter of Alexander II to the President of the United States
August 17, 1866

"I have received by the hands of Mr. Fox the resolution of the Congress of the United States of America on the occasion of the Providential favor of which I have been the object. This mark of sympathy has touched me deeply. It is not merely personal to me, - it is a new attestation of the sentiments which unite the American nation to Russia. ...These cordial relations, which are as advantageous to their reciprocal interests as to those of civilization and humanity, conform to the view of Divine Providence, whose final purpose is peace and concord among nations. It is with a lively satisfaction that I see these bonds continually strengthening.

I have communicated my sentiments to Mr. Fox. I pray you to express them to Congress and to the American people, of which that body is the organ. Tell them how much I – and with me all Russia – appreciate the testimonials of friendship which they have given me, and how heartily I shall congratulate myself on seeing the American nation growing in power and prosperity by the union and continued practice of the civic virtues which distinguish it.

Accept, at the same time, the assurance of the high consideration with which I am

Your good friend,
Alexander

U.S. National Archives and Records Administration

6. This Russian interior report details the warm welcome given to Fox on his visit to the city of Kostroma during his mission to Russia in 1867.

The Report of Staff Captain Andreyev to the Chief of the Third Department of His Majesty's Own Chancellery, Shuvalov, on the visit of the American Delegation in Kostroma August 24, 1866

"Upon their arrival to dinner, the dear friends were greeted by the American anthem at the entrance and, when they had entered the dining hall, children wearing their holiday clothes greeted them with bouquets of flowers and welcoming words in English. . . .National and American flags decorated the outside of the Hall of the Nobility . . . Inside the building were large trees, flowers and huge American flags and banners with the names of Johnson, Washington and Lincoln."

State Archive of the Russian Federation, Moscow

7. Grand Duke Alexis, son of Alexander II, was entertained everywhere with great enthusiasm during his official visit to the United States in 1871-72. In this letter to his mother, he describes some of his impressions.

Letter of Grand Duke Alexis Alexandrovich to his Mother, Empress Marie Alexandrovna, written during his visit to America.
January-February 3, 1872

"I was astounded by the number of beautiful women in New York and St. Louis. With regard to my success among the American ladies that was written up so much in the newspapers, I can tell you sincerely that it is complete nonsense.

23 January: We are going to Louisville, one of the arch-enemies of the Northern States during the war, and I can tell you that I am surprised by their invitation, since we had always supported the North – that is we were against the Southern States. Despite that, they are still inviting us. A wonderful reception and a ball in Louisville, as usual…. Here, they are more like the Europeans . . . very similar to our old nobility…

On Tuesday, we are departing for New Orleans on a steamship along the Mississippi… New Orleans leaves a completely European impression, since all people and high society speak in French…"

State Archive of the Russian Federation, Moscow

8. One of the definitive events of the era of the Tsar and the President, was the sale of Russia's North American colony, later named Alaska, to the United States in 1867. This message of de Stoeckl to Seward confirms the authorization of Alexander II to proceed with the sale.

Dispatch of the Russian Envoy to the United States E.A. Stoeckl to Secretary of State William H. Seward on the sale of Alaska
March 17/29, 1867

"I have the honor to inform you that by a telegram dated March 16/28 of this month from St. Petersburg, Prince Gorchakov informs me that His Majesty, the Emperor of all the Russias, gives his consent to the cession of the Russian possessions on the American continent in the United States for the stipulated sum of seven million two hundred thousand dollars in gold, and that His Majesty, the Emperor, invests me with full powers to negotiate and sign the treaty. Please accept, Mr. Secretary of State, the assurance of my very high consideration.

STOECKL*"*

U.S. National Archives and Records Administration

9. Mark Twain, America's famed humorist author, paid a courtesy call on Alexander II at Livadia, the Tsar's Crimean villa on the Black Sea near Yalta in the course of a voyage through Europe and the Middle East. His impression of Alexander II is described in his 1869 publication, *The Innocents Abroad*.

"The Emperor wore a cap, frock coat and pantaloons. No jewelry or insignia whatever of rank. No costume could be less ostentatious. He is very tall and spare and a determined looking man, though a very pleasant one, nevertheless. It is easy to see that he is kind and affectionate. There is something very noble in his expression when the cap is off....

After the U.S. Consul's opening address which the Tsar bore with unflinching fortitude . . . he thanked us for the address and said he was much pleased to see us, especially as such friendly relations existed between Russia and the United States. The Empress said the Americans were favorites in Russia, and she hoped the Russians were similarly regarded in America. These were all the speeches that were made, and I recommend them to parties who present police with gold watches as models of brevity and point."

The Innocents Abroad by Mark Twain, 1869 (publisher to be inserted)

Checklist of Objects

Alexander II

1. **Portrait of Emperor Alexander II**
   A.A. Harlamov, 1874
   Oil on canvas
   State Historical Museum, Moscow

2. **Flag of Imperial Russia**
   ca 1860s

3. **View of the Kremlin toward the Spassky Gate**
   Engraving from the watercolor by G.M. Lori
   Early 19th century
   State Historical Museum, Moscow

4. **Room in the Nicholas Palace of the Kremlin where Grand Duke Alexander Nicholaevich was born**
   Watercolor from the original by P. Zaitsev, 1836
   State Historical Museum, Moscow

5. **Portrait of Grand Duke Alexander Nicholaevich as an infant**
   Unknown artist, 1830s
   Oil on canvas
   State Historical Museum, Moscow

6. **Measurement icon of Blessed Prince St. Alexander Nevsky**
   St. Petersburg, 1840s
   Wood, oil on canvas, silver, gilding
   State Historical Museum, Moscow

   Icon of the patron saint of the future Alexander II, measuring the length of the infant Tsarevich at birth, as was the tradition.

7. **Portrait of Grand Duchess Alexandra Feodorovna, mother of Grand Duke Alexander Nicholaevich, the future Alexander II**
   Alexander Molinari, ca 1810
   Oil on canvas
   State Historical Museum, Moscow

8. **Portrait of Grand Duke Nicholas Pavlovich, future Nicholas I, father of Grand Duke Alexander Nicholaevich,**
   Unknown artist, from the original by O.A. Kiprenski,
   Mid- 19th century
   Oil on canvas
   State Historical Museum, Moscow

9. **Case with the Official Service Record of Tsarevich, Grand Duke Alexander Nicholaevich**
   St. Petersburg, 1 January 1850
   Glass case with gilded metal
   Leather folio with gilded imprint
   State Historical Museum, Moscow

10. **Coffeepot with the image of Tsarevich Alexander II Nikolaevich**
    Russia, Zh'ell porcelain factory, late 1820s-early 1830s
    Porcelain, painting, gilding
    State Historical Museum, Moscow

    Cup and saucer with the image of Tsarevich Alexander Nikolaevich
    Russia, Zh'ell porcelain factory, late 1820s-early 1830s
    Porcelain, painting, gilding
    State Historical Museum, Moscow

    Cup and saucer with the image of Tsarevich Alexander Nikolaevich
    Russia, Safronov factory, late 1820s-early 1830s
    Porcelain, painting, gilding
    State Historical Museum, Moscow

13. **Portrait of Tsarevich Alexander Nicholaevich**
Vologda, 1838
Work master, S. Skripitsyn
Silver, niello, wood, copper, gilding
State Historical Museum, Moscow

14. **Catechism presented to Tsarevich Alexander Nicholaevich at Easter, 1822**
April 2, 1822
Leather, gilding
Manuscript with original pencil and watercolor drawings
State Archive of the Russian Federation, Moscow

15. **Easter egg with a miniature of the Madonna and Child with angels**
St. Petersburg, 1860s-80s
Imperial Porcelain Factory
Porcelain and biscuit with relief modeling in the style of Wedgwood
Raymond F. Piper Collection

16. **Easter egg with angels and the Christ Child with orb St. Petersburg, 1860s-70s**
Imperial Porcelain Factory
Porcelain and biscuit with relief modeling in the style of Wedgwood
Raymond F. Piper Collection

17. **Portrait of Vassily Andreevich Zhukovsky**
Lithograph
A.I. Lebedev from the original by F. Kruger, 1869
State Historical Museum, Moscow

Renowned Russian poet and tutor of Alexander II

18. **Portrait of Karl K. Merder**
Watercolor
M. Gradovskaya, copy of the original, 1834
State Historical Museum, Moscow

Tutor of Alexander II in military science

19. **Notebook of Tsarevich Alexander Nicholaevich (English vocabulary) 1827**
Cover inscribed by the Tsarevich:
"Vocabulary of English words and phrases. No.1 A.N. 1827"
State Archive of the Russian Federation, Moscow

20. **Notebook of Tsarevich Alexander Nicholaevich with excerpts from the works of English writers, 1830-1832**
In English
Hand-written, ink, pencil, leather binding, embossed
State Archive of the Russian Federation, Moscow

21. **Notebook of Tsarevich Alexander Nicholaevich of French phrases translated into English, 1828**
Cover inscribed by the Tsarevich:
"No. 1. Eng. Translation. A.N. February 22, 1878"
State Archive of the Russian Federation, Moscow

22. **Notebook of Tsarevich Alexander Nicholaevich on English poetery, 1828**
Cover inscribed by the Tsarevich:
"No. 1. English poetry. A.N. 1828"
State Archive of the Russian Federation, Moscow

23. **Report on the character of Tsarevich Alexander Nicholaevich by his tutor, Karl Merder**
January 1833
Hand-written
State Archive of the Russian Federation, Moscow

24. **Portrait of Tsarevich Alexander Nicholaevich**
P.F.Sokolov, 1829
Watercolor
State Archive of the Russian Federation, Moscow

25. **Double portrait of Tsarevich Alexander Nicholaevich and Grand Duke Konstantin Nicholaevich 1835**
W.K.Hau
Pencil drawing
State Archive of the Russian Federation, Moscow

26. **Gala dinner in honor of the Coming of Age of Tsarevich Alexander Nicholaevich hosted by D.I. Naryshkin in St.Petersburg**
Unknown artist, Russia 1834
Oil on canvas
State Historical Museum, Moscow

27. **Oath of Loyalty of Tsarevich Alexander Nicholaevich to Nicholas I**
Signed: "Alexander"
St. Petersburg, 22 April 1834
Paper, printing, ink
State Historical Museum, Moscow

28. **Pipe in a case with the images of Emperor Nicholas I and Tsarevich Alexander Nicholaevich**
Vienna, Austria, 1836
Meerschaum, wood, leather, kid-skin, brass, steel, carving
State Historical Museum, Moscow

29. **Portrait of Empress Marie Alexandrovna, wife of Alexander II**
T.A. Neff, 1864, copy of the portrait by Winterhalter
Oil on canvas
State Historical Museum, Moscow

30. **Pieces from the Wedding Service of Tsarevich Alexander Nicholaevich**
Soup plate, gravy server, wine cooler, platter
St. Petersburg, Imperial Porcelain Factory, 1841
Porcelain, painting, gilding
State Historical Museum, Moscow

31. **Pocket watch with portraits of Alexander II and Marie Alexandrovna**
Geneva, mid-19th century, Chapek and C.
Gold, enamel, metal, glass
State Historical Museum, Moscow

32. **Wallet of shell with photographs of Alexander II and Empress Marie Alexandrovna**
Germany/Russia, 1870s
Mother- of-pearl, silk, leather, white metal alloy, photo prints
State Historical Museum, Moscow

33. **The Zubov Wing of the Grand Palace, Tsarskoye Selo**
Luigi Premazzi, 1855
Watercolor
State Museum-Preserve, "Tsarskoye Selo", St.Petersburg

34. **The Dressing Room of Tsarevich Alexander Nicholaevich in the Grand Palace, Tsarskoye Selo**
Edward Hau, 1850
Watercolor
State Museum- Preserve, "Tsarskoye Selo", St. Petersburg

35. **Easter egg with a miniature of the Apostle Peter**
St. Petersburg, 1850s-60s
Imperial Porcelain Factory
Raymond F. Piper Collection

The miniature is from the icon painting of St. Peter by T.A. Neff on the iconostasis in St. Isaac's Cathedral, St. Petersburg

36. **Small icon of the Guardian Angel**
St. Petersburg, S.Arndt, 1840-70
Silver, mother-of-pearl, painting, gilding
State Museum- Preserve "Tsarskoye Selo", St.Petersburg

From the rooms of Alexander II

37. **Small icon of the Virgin of Kazan**
Moscow, 1860s
Silver, wood, oil, velvet
State Museum- Preserve "Tsarskoye Selo", St. Petersburg

From the rooms of Alexander II

38. **Small icon of St. Mitrofan**
Voronezh, 1837
Silver, mica, fabric, gilding, painting, engraving
State Museum-Preserve "Tsarskoye Selo"

From the rooms of Alexander II

39. **Small icon of St. Iakov and St. Dmitry of Rostov**
Russia, 1840-1870
Silver, enamel, painting, gilding
State Museum- Preserve "Tsarskoye Selo", St. Petersburg

From the rooms of Alexander II

40. **The Turkish Room in the Grand Palace, Tsarskoye Selo**
Philip Steinmuller, 1850s
Watercolor
State Museum- Preserve "Tsarskoye Selo", St. Petersburg

41. **Traite de la langue Arabe vulgaire**
Book by Sheik Muhammed Ayad-el-Tantavy
Leipzig, 1848
Morocco leather, gold embossing, moiré
Interior inscription by the author
State Museum - Preserve "Tsarskoye Selo"

A manual of the Arab language, in French and Arabic, presented to Alexander II while still Tsarevich. From the library of Alexander II

42. **Cigarette container**
19th c
Silver, garnet, chasing, gilding
State Museum- Preserve "Tsarskoye Selo", St. Petersburg

From the rooms of Alexander II

43. **Incidents in my Life**
Book, by D.D. Home
London, 1864
Inscription by the author to Alexander II outside the cover
State Museum-Preserve "Tsarskoye Selo", St. Petersburg

The author relates his visit to Peterhof Palace in 1858 at the invitation of Alexander II

From the library of Alexander II

44. **The Mirror Study of Marie Alexandrovna in the Grand Palace, Tsarskoye Selo**
Edward Hau, 1860s
Watercolor
State Museum- Preserve "Tsarskoye Selo", St. Petersburg

45. **Tete - a - tete tea set of Empress Marie Alexandrovna**
St. Petersburg, 1860s
Imperial Porcelain Factory
Tray, teapot, creamer, sugar bowl, two cups and saucrs
Celadon with gilded Imperial crown and the cypher of Empress Marie Alexandrovna
Raymond F. Piper Collection

46. **Portrait of Empress Marie Alexandrovna**
Alois Gustav Rockstuhl, 1862
Watercolor, frame: bronze, velvet
State Museum- Preserve "Tsarskoye Selo", St. Petersburg

47. **Portrait of Emperor Alexander II**
Alois Gustav Rockstuhl
Watercolor, frame: wood, brass
State Museum- Preserve "Tsarskoye Selo", St. Petersburg

48. **Case with inset box of game chips**
France, 1850s
Maple, bronze, porcelain, mother-of-pearl, gilding
State Museum- Preserve "Tsarskoye Selo", St. Petersburg

49. **Inkwell**
France, J. Petit factories, 1850s
Porcelain, modeling, relief, polychrome painting, gilding
State Museum- Preserve "Tsarskoye Selo", St. Petersburg

From the rooms of Alexander II

50. **Favorites of the Emperor's family (pets)**
Johann Schwabe, 1867
Oil on canvas
State Museum- Preserve "Tsarskoye Selo", St. Petersburg

51. **Outing of Grand Duchess Marie Alexandrovna**
Franz Teichel, 1858
Watercolor
State Museum- Preserve "Tsarskoye Selo", St. Petersburg

The young daughter of Alexander II is seen riding in a carriage with her attendants along the paths of the park at Tsarskoye Selo

52. **Children's Island in the Alexander Park, Tsarskoye Selo**
Carl Kollman, 1820s
Lithograph
State Museum-Preserve "Tsarskoye Selo", St. Petersburg

53. **Alexander II and his grandson, Grand Duke Nicholas Alexandrovich, the future Nicholas II**
Adolphe Charlemagne, 1876
Watercolor
State Museum-Preserve "Tsarskoye Selo", St. Petersburg

54. **Desk frame with photograph of Grand Duchess Marie Alexandrovna**
St. Petersburg, studio of G. Denyer, 1870s
Frame: bronze, lazurite, glass, gilding, color tinted
State Museum- Preserve "Tsarskoye Selo"

Grand Duchess Marie, daughter of Alexander II and Marie Alexandrovna, married Prince Alfred, son of Queen Victoria, in 1874 and became Duchess of Edinburgh.

From the personal belongings of Alexander II and Marie Alexandrovna

55. **Popular print of a photograph of Alexander II with his family**
Chromolithograph, 1877
State Archive of the Russian Federation, Moscow

56. **Portrait of Alexander II with his wife, Empress Marie Alexandrovna**
Color tinted photograph by F.V. Morozov, Moscow, 1870
State Archive of the Russian Federation, Moscow

57. **Portrait of Grand Duchess Marie Alexandrovna (daughter of Alexander II)**
Otto Donher von Richter, 1872
Oil on canvas
State Historical Museum, Moscow

58. **Portrait of Grand Duke Nicholas Alexandrovich in the winter jacket of the Grodno Hussar Life Guards**
Georg Bothman, 1868
Oil on canvas
State Museum-Preserve "Tsarskoye Selo", St. Petersburg

The eldest son and heir of Alexander II, who died of spinal meningitis at the age of twenty-one.

59. **Portrait of Tsarevich, Grand Duke Alexander Alexandrovich in the uniform of a general of the Chevalier Guards**
Sergei Zaryanko, 1867
Oil on canvas
State Museum- Preserve "Tsarskoye Selo", St. Petersburg

As the second son of Alexander II, he succeeded his deceased brother as Tsarevich. He became Alexander III on the death of his father in 1881.

60. **Portrait of Grand Duke Sergei Alexandrovich**
Ivan Kramskoy, 1870
Watercolor
State Museum- Preserve "Tsarskoye Selo",, St. Petersburg

Grand Duke Serge was the fifth son of Alexander II who later became Governor-General of Moscow. In 1905, he was assassinated by a terrorist bomb.

61. **Portrait of Grand Duke Paul Alexandrovich**
Ivan Kramskoy, 1870
Watercolor
State Museum- Preserve "Tsarskoye Selo", St. Petersburg

Grand Duke Paul was the youngest son of Alexander II. He was imprisoned by the Bolsheviks and executed in the Peter and Paul Fortress in 1919.

62. **Ceremonial entry of Alexander II into Moscow on Blvd. Tverskaya for the coronation**
Unknown artist
Oil on canvas
State Historical Museum, Moscow

63. **Proclamation of the coronation by heralds on Red Square**
Chromolithograph by Lemercier after the original by M. Zichy
Collection of Lacey R. Greer, Treasures of Imperial Russia

64. **Announcement of the coronation of Alexander II and Marie Alexandrovna**
Lithograph, workshop of A. Petersen
St. Petersburg, August 26, 1856
State Historical Museum, Moscow

65. **Cigarette case with a view of the Moscow Kremlin**
Moscow, 1857
Gilded silver, niello
State Historical Museum, Moscow

66. **Emperor Alexander II in coronation robes**
Chromolithograph from the original by an unknown artist, 1850s
State Historical Museum, Moscow

67. **Empress Marie Alexandrovna in coronation robes**
Chromolithograph from the original by an unknown artist, 1850s
State Historical Museum, Moscow

68. **Anointing of Emperor Alexander II by Metropolitan Filaret during the coronation in the Uspensky Cathedral of the Kremlin, August 26, 1856**
Lithograph
V.F. Timm, 1856
State Historical Museum, Moscow

69. **Portrait of Metropolitan Filaret of Moscow in coronation vestments**
N.E. Rachkov, 1857
Oil on canvas
State Historical Museum, Moscow

69. **Alexander II placing the crown on the head of Empress Marie Alexandrovna during the coronation**
Chromolithograph by Lemercier after the original by V.F. Timm
Collection of Lacey R. Greer, Treasures of Imperial Russia

70. **Festive procession of Emperor Alexander II through Ivanov Square in the Moscow Kremlin after the coronation in the Uspensky Cathedral**
G. Schwartz, 1856
Oil on canvas
State Historical Museum, Moscow

71. **Illumination of Moscow on the occasion of the accession to the throne of Alexander II, 1856**
V. Sadovnikov, 1856
Watercolor
State Museum-Preserve "Tsarskoye Selo", St. Petersburg

72. **Menu of a gala dinner during the coronation celebrations in Moscow**
September 2, 1856
Chromolithograph
St. Petersburg, workshop of A. Petersen, 1856
State Historical Museum, Moscow

73. **Façade of the Grand Palace, Tsarskoye Selo**
V. Sadovnikov, 1860s
Watercolor
State Museum- Preserve "Tsarskoye Selo", St. Petersburg

74. **Portrait of Alexander II wearing a tunic of His Majesty's Hussar Regiment of Household Troops**
Nikolai Lavrov, 1860
Oil on canvas
State Museum- Preserve "Tsarskoye Selo", St. Petersburg

75. **Military plate with a scene of officers of the Finnish Artillery Battalion**
St. Petersburg, 1850s-60s
Imperial Porcelain Factory
Raymond F. Piper Collection

76. **Military plate with a scene of officers of the Grodno Hussar Regiment**
St. Petersburg, 1850s-60s
Imperial Porcelain Factory
Raymond F. Piper Collection

77. **St. George silver trumpet with the ribbon of the Order of St. George**
St. Petersburg, late 19th c
Silver, moiré, silver thread, engraving
State Historical Museum, Moscow

Inscription on the bell of the trumpet:To the Battalion of the 12th Astrakhan Grenadier Regiment of H.I.H. Tsarevich Alexander for defeating and capturing the Turkish Army at Pleven"

78. **Tunic of a General of the Grodno Hussar Life Guards Regiment**
Russia, 1877
Broadcloth, silk, silver lace, silver braid
Inscription on the lining:"From Her Majesty, April 17, 1877"
State Museum- Preserve "Tsarskoye Selo", St. Petersburg

Belonged to Alexander II

79. **Aiguillette with shoulder strap of a general of the Grodno Hussar Life Guards Regiment**
Russia, 1877
Silver braid, metal
State Museum-Preserve "Tsarskoye Selo", St. Petersburg

Belonged to Alexander II

80. **Folding chair**
Russia, 1860-1870
Wood, leather, metal
State Historical Museum, Moscow

Inscription on a plaque at the foot of the chair: "Traveling chair of Emperor Alexander II; which was used by him during the War with Turkey, 1877 – 1878"

81. **The Study of Alexander II in the Grand Palace, Tsarskoye Selo**
Edward Hau, 1857
Watercolor
State Museum- Preserve "Tsarskoye Selo", St. Petersburg

82. **Desk clock in the form of a Gothic cathedral**
Austria, before 1845
Bronze, mother-of-pearl, wood, glass, metal, enamel, steel, painting, gilding
State Museum- Preserve "Tsarskoye Selo", St. Petersburg

From the study of Alexander II in the Grand Palace, Tsarskoye Selo

83. **Desk set**
Russia, 1826-1845
Mother-of-pearl, bronze, wood, velvet, gilding
State Museum- Preserve "Tsarskoye Selo", St. Petersburg

From the personal belongings of Alexander II

84. **Desk model of the monument commemorating the Millennium of Rus'**
St. Petersburg, Peterhof Lapidary Works, 1860s
Bronze, marble
State Museum- Preserve "Tsarskoye Selo", St. Petersburg

Model of the monument erected in Novgorod in 1862 for the celebration of the millennium of Rus' initiated by Alexander II

From the rooms of Alexander II in the Grand Palace, Tsarskoye Selo

85. **Framed photograph of Empress Marie Alexandrovna**
Photograph
St. Petersburg, mid-19th c
Hand painted retouching
Frame: Vienna, K. Kellerman Factory
Bronze, glass
State Museum- Preserve "Tsarskoye Selo", St. Petersburg

From the rooms of Alexander II in the Grand Palace, Tsarskoye Selo

86. **Icon of the Virgin of Smolensk**
     Moscow, Firm of Sazikov, 1854
     Silver, enamel, sapphires, rubies, wood, tempera,
     gilding
     State Historical Museum, Moscow

     Belonged to Alexander II

87. **Cigarette case**
     Russia, 3rd quarter of the 19th c
     Velvet, leather, silk, straw, metal, wickerwork
     State Museum- Preserve "Tsarskoye Selo", St.
     Petersburg

     From the rooms of Alexander II

88. **Chibouk holder**
     Russia, mid-19th c
     Amber, wood, aventurine
     State Museum- Preserve "Tsarskoye Selo", St.
     Petersburg

     From the personal belongings of Alexander II

89. **Briefcase**
     England. 2nd half of the 19th c
     Leather, cardboard, metal
     Scissors, inkwell, cylinder case for paper
     State Museum- Preserve "Tsarskoye Selo", St.
     Petersburg

     From the personal belongings of Alexander II

90. **Framed photograph of Alexander II in his study
     in the Winter Palace**
     St. Petersburg, 1870s
     Photograph
     Frame: wood, metal, velvet
     State Museum- Preserve "Tsarskoye Selo", St.
     Petersburg

     *From the rooms of Alexander II in the Grand Palace,
     Tsarskoye Selo*

91. **Portrait of Prince Alexander M. Gorchakov**
     I.P. Keller-Villiamdi, 1867
     Oil on canvas
     State Historical Museum, Moscow

92. **Portrait-badge with portraits of Emperors
     Alexander II and Alexander III**
     Russia, 2nd half of the 19th c
     Gold, silver, diamonds, quartz, glass, tempera,
     painting
     State Historical Museum, Moscow

     Thought to have belonged to Prince A. Gorchakov

93. **Letter of Alexander II to the US President**
     February 20, 1855
     U.S. National Archives and Records
     Administration

     *At the beginning of his reign, asking the US to continue
     the same consideration that was given to his father,
     Nicholas I*

94. **Letter of Alexander II to President Lincoln**
     September 21, 1860
     U.S. National Archives and Records
     Administration

     *Announcing the birth of a son, Grand Duke Paul
     Alexandrovich*

95. **Official copy of a letter of President Lincoln to
     Alexander II**
     April 8, 1861
     U.S. National Archives and Records
     Administration

     *Announcing the recall of the American envoy, John
     Appleton*

96. **Letter of Alexander II to President Lincoln**
     June 28, 1861
     U.S. National Archives and Records
     Administration

     *Reply to the recall of the American envoy, John
     Appleton*

97. **Letter of Alexander II to President Lincoln**
     July 6, 1862
     U.S. National Archives and Records
     Administration

     *Announcing the birth of a son to his brother, Grand
     Duke Konstantin*

98. **Draft of a letter of President Lincoln to Alexander II**
September 6, 1862
U.S. National Archives and Records
Administration

Lincoln's hand-written reply with good wishes on the birth of the newly born Prince Vyacheslav

99. **Letter of Alexander II to the President**
July 1865
U.S. National Archives and Records
Administration

Announcing the death of his son and heir, Tsarevich Nicholas Alexandrovich

100. **Letter of a US citizen to Alexander II**
April 1878
Hand-written with envelope
State Archive of the Russian Federation, Moscow

101. **Letter of American citizen C.W. Ford to Alexander II**
Philadelphia, March 26, 1880
State Archive of the Russian Federation, Moscow

102. **Envelope of a letter of a US citizen to Alexander II**
December 1878
State Archive of the Russian Federation, Moscow

103. **Presentation ring with a portrait of Alexander II**
Russia, 1855-1881
Gold, silver, rock crystal, ivory, gouache
State Historical Museum, Moscow

104. **Bas-relief of Emperor Alexander II**
Russia, 1866
Porcelain, biscuit, relief, gilding
State Historical Museum, Moscow

105. **Menu of a Naval dinner at Kronstadt in honor of the arrival of the American delegation headed by Gustavus V. Fox in July 1866**
Kronstadt, July 28, 1866
Chromolithograph, A.I. Charlemagne
St. Petersburg, lithography shop of A. Petersen
In Russian and French
State Historical Museum, Moscow

106. **Menu of a dinner in honor of Gustavus V. Fox and the American delegation given by Moscow Governor-General, Prince V.A. Dolgoruky**
Moscow, August 12, 1866
Chromolithograph, I.I. Charlemagne
State Historical Museum, Moscow

107. **Report of the Staff Captain Andreyev to the Head of the Third Department of His Majesty's Own Chancellery, Shuvalov, on the visit of the American delegation to Kostroma**
August 24, 1866
Hand-written
State Archive of the Russian Federation, Moscow

108. **Menu of a dinner in honor of Gustavus V. Fox and the American delegation given by Moscow Governor-General, Prince V.A. Dolgoruky**
Moscow, August 30, 1866
Chromolithograph, I.I. Charlemagne
State Historical Museum,, Moscow

109. **Itinerary of Grand Duke Alexis Alexandrovich on his visit to the United States of America**
Printed copy
In Russian and English
State Archive of the Russian Federation, Moscow

110. **Photograph of Grand Duke Alexis Alexandrovich**
M.B. Brandy
Washington, DC, Library of Congress, 1871
State Archive of the Russian Federation, Moscow

111. **Telegram of Grand Duke Alexis to his father, Alexander II, sent during his visit to the United States**
Memphis, February 5, 1872
In French
State Archive of the Russian Federation, Moscow

112. **Letter of Grand Duke Alexis Alexandrovich to his mother, Empress Marie Alexandrovna, during his visit to America**
January-February 3, 1872
Hand-written
State Archive of the Russian Federation, Moscow

113. **Letter of Grand Duke Alexis Alexandrovich to his mother, Empress Marie Alexandrovna, during his visit to America**
New York, April 2, 1872
Hand-written on personal stationery
State Archive of the Russian Federation, Moscow

114. **Visit of Grand Duke Alexis to Milwaukee, January 1872**
London, 1874
Red morocco leather, gilding, gold embossing
State Museum- Preserve "Tsarskoye Selo", St. Petersburg
Album depicting the visit of the Grand Duke, son of Alexander II, to Milwaukee during his official visit to the United States
From the library of Alexander II

115. **Box of Grand Duke Alexis Alexandrovich**
St. Petersburg, 1880-1890
Firm of Faberge: workmaster J. Rappoport
Silver, engraving, gilding
State Historical Museum, Moscow

116. **Portrait of Alexander II**
Ivan Tyurin, 1874
Oil on canvas
State Museum- Preserve "Tsarskoye Selo", St. Petersburg

117. **Portrait of Grand Duke Konstantin Nicholaevich (brother of Alexander II)**
Unknown artist, 1850s
Oil on canvas
State Historical Museum, Moscow

118. **Document of a sale of serfs with their wives and children for 1485 roubles**
Simbirsk, February 1, 1806
State Historical Museum, Moscow

119. **Outline of the speech of Alexander II on the Liberation of Peasants from serfdom**
1861
Original with autograph
Pencil
State Archive of the Russian Federation, Moscow

120. **Speech of Alexander II at the General Assembly of the State Council at the opening of a meeting devoted to reviewing the main provisions of the liberation of peasants from serfdom**
January 28, 1861
Hand-written
State Archive of the Russian Federation, Moscow

121. **Draft of the Manifesto of Alexander II on the abolition of serfdom**
No later than January 24, 1861
State Archive of the Russian Federation, Moscow

122. **Manifesto of Alexander II on the liberation of peasants from serfdom**
February 19, 1861
Printed copy
State Historical Museum, Moscow

123. **General Provision on Peasants freed from serfdom**
February 19, 1861
Printed copy
State Archive of the Russian Federation, Moscow

124. **Folk embroidery tea set**
St. Petersburg, 1870s
Imperial Porcelain Factory
Teapot, creamer, sugar bowl with lid, tea cup and saucer, footed bowl, cover saucer
Raymond F. Piper Collection

125. **Reading of the Manifesto of February 19, 1861 in the Assumption Cathedral of the Moscow Kremlin on March 5, 1861. Room in the Cadet Barracks where the meetings of the Reviewing Commssions on the preparation of the abolition of serfdom were held**
Chromolithograph, V.F. Timm, 1861
State Historical Museum, Moscow

126. **Reading of the Manifesto on the liberation of peasants at a landowner's estate**
Chromolithograph, V.F. Timm, 1861
State Historical Museum, Moscow

127. **Russian peasants thanking Alexander II for their liberation from serfdom**
Chromolithograph after the original by B. Rozhansky
A.Belozerov publication, 1860s
State Historical Museum, Moscow

128. **"The Unforgettable Day of the Emancipation of Peasants from serfdom on February 19, 1861: Glory to the Tsar-Liberator!"**
Popular print
Lithograph by Peter Lukyanov, Moscow, 1861
State Archive of the Russian Federation, Moscow

129. **Portrait of the "Tsar-Liberator" Alexander II**
Phototype portrait created from more than 12,000 words of the Manifesto liberating the serfs, and main events of his reign
Hand drawn in ink by V. Malyushitsky
L. Kototulov, publisher, St. Petersburg, late 19th century
State Historical Museum, Moscow

130. **Portrait of Alexander II wearing the uniform of a general**
Oil on canvas
Pavel Antonov, 1875
State Museum- Preserve "Tsarskoye Selo", St. Petersburg

131. **"Commemoration of the 60th birthday of the Sovereign Emperor Alexander Nicholaevich, Tsar of All the Russias"**
1879
Popular print, chromolithograph by Abramov, Moscow
State Archive of the Russian Federation, Moscow

132. **Alexander II riding in a sleigh along the Neva embankment, 1881**
Barclay de Tolly (Weimarn), 1881
Oil on canvas
State Museum- Preserve "Tsarskoye Selo", St. Petersburg

133. **"The Sovereign Alexander II visiting Grand Duchess Ekaterina Mikhailovna following a review at the Mikhailovsky Manege on March 1, 1881"**
Engraving by A. Shlipper
St. Petersburg, 1881
State Historical Museum, Moscow

134. **Attempt on the life of Alexander II. Explosion of the second bomb, March 1, 1881**
From the original by A. Baldniger
Moscow, 1881
State Historical Museum, Moscow

135. **Last minutes of the life of Emperor Alexander II**
A.Lebedev, 1881
Paper, ink, pencil
State Historical Museum, Moscow

136. **Spiritual Will and Testament of Alexander II**
Livadia, September 8, 1876
Handwritten
State Archive of the Russian Federation, Moscow

137. **Alexander II in death**
Unknown artist, 1880s
Oil on canvas
State Historical Museum, Moscow

138. **Pamphlet announcing the "execution" of Alexander II by the "People's Will" party on March 1, 1881**
St. Petersburg, March 2, 1881
Paper, typographic print
State Historical Museum, Moscow

139. **Cross made from a shard of the window glass from the carriage in which Alexander II was riding on March 1, 1881**
Russia, 1881
Glass, case of leather, velvet, silk
State Historical Museum, Moscow

140. **"The sorrowful carriage." Transfer of the body of the Sovereign Emperor from the Winter Palace to the Peter and Paul Cathedral**
1881
Popular print, color lithograph by F.V. Morozov, Moscow
State Archive of the Russian Federation, Moscow

141. **"The demise of His Imperial Majesty, the Sovereign Emperor Alexander II. Catafalque in the palace church"**
1881
Popular print, color lithograph by I.D. Sytin, Moscow
State Archive of the Russian Federation

142. **"The demise of His Imperial Majesty, the Sovereign Emperor Alexander II. View of the location where the attempt on the life of His Majesty took place"**
1881
Popular print, lithograph by V.V. Ponomaryov, Moscow 1881
State Archive of the Russian Federation, Moscow

143. **Mourning ring with the image of Emperor Alexander II**
Russia, ca 1881
Gold, enamel
State Historical Museum, Moscow

144. **Uniform of a General-Adjutant, 1880-1881**
Russia, early 1880-1881
Tunic with epaulettes
Broadcloth, silk, gold and silver embroidery, metal, gilding
State Historical Museum, Moscow

Belonged to Alexander III; he wore this uniform at the funeral of his father, Alexander II, on March 15, 1881

145. **Portrait of Grand Duke Alexander Alexandrovich (future Emperor Alexander III)**
Oil on canvas
I.A. Tyurin, ca 1865
State Historical Museum, Moscow

146. **Expression of the people's sorrow in memory of the Tsar-Liberator and Martyr who fell at the hands of evil-doers on March 1, 1881**
Popular print, chromolithograph by A. Streltsov, Moscow
State Archive of the Russian Federation, Moscow

147. **Photograph of N.I. Rysakov, a participant in the assassination of Alexander II on March 1, 1881**
Photograph on a postcard
State Archive of the Russian Federation, Moscow

148. **Photograph of S.L. Perovskaya, one of the leaders of the People's Will organization**
Photograph
State Archive of the Russian Federation, Moscow

149. **St. Petersburg. Church of the Resurrection of Christ (Saviour on the Blood) built on the site of the lethal wounding of Alexander II**
Color autotype, c 1910
State Historical Museum, Moscow

150 **"Two unforgettable feats of Alexander II"**
Chromolithograph, P.I. Orekhov, 1878
State Historical Museum, Moscow

151. **Pair of commemorative plates with the images of Emperor Alexander II and Empress Marie Alexandrovna**
St. Petersburg. Imperial Porcelain Factory, ca 1881
Porcelain, painting, gilding
State Historical Museum, Moscow

152. **Bas-relief of Emperor Alexander II**
Russia, 1866
Marble in porcelain frame
State Historical Museum, Moscow

153. **Mourning ring on the death of Emperor Alexander II**
Russia, 1881
Gold, enamel
State Historical Museum, Moscow

Abraham Lincoln

154. **Chair from the Lincoln White House**
Wood, fabric, horsehair
Ca. 1860-1865
National Park Service, Ford's Theatre National
Historic Site

155. **Head of Abraham Lincoln**
Plaster, paint
Vinnie Ream, 1866
National Park Service, Ford's Theatre National
Historic Site

156. **Abraham Lincoln**
Oil on canvas
F.G. Strieby, 1887
National Park Service, Ford's Theatre National
Historic Site

157. **Passport of Cassius Marcellus Clay**
1863
Abraham Lincoln Library and Museum at Lincoln
Memorial University, Harrogate, TN

158. **Le Prince Alexandre Gortchacow**
Lithograph
Based on a photograph by Deniere, lithograph by
C. Schultz, Lemercier, Paris,
J. Velten, St Petersbourg & Carlesruhe
Ca. 1865
Seward House Museum, Auburn, NY

159. **Telegram of Cassius Clay to Montgomery Blair**
March 27, 1861
Library of Congress

160. **William Seward to Abraham Lincoln**
September 7, 1861
Library of Congress

161. **Diplomatic Party Excursion of de Stoeckl &
Seward, Saratoga Springs**
Photograph
Photographer unknown, August 1863
Seward House Museum, Auburn, NY

161. **USS Miantonomoh, St. John's, Newfoundland**
ca. 1866-1867
Naval Historical Center

162. **Speech of Cassius M. Clay in English and
Russian**
Wynkoop, Hallenbeck & Thomas, New York, 1863
Abraham Lincoln Library and Museum at Lincoln
Memorial University, Harrogate, TN

163. **George W. Morgan, Lisbon, to Cassius M. Clay**
June 11, 1861
Abraham Lincoln Library and Museum at Lincoln
Memorial University, Harrogate, TN

164. **John Appleton, Washington, to Hon. C.M. Clay**
September 22, 1861
Abraham Lincoln Library and Museum at Lincoln
Memorial University, Harrogate, TN

165. **Edward Everett, Boston, to C.M. Clay**
October 29, 1861
Abraham Lincoln Library and Museum at Lincoln
Memorial University, Harrogate, TN

166. **Letter of Prince Gortchacow, St. Petersburg, to
Mr. Clay**
February 14, 1862
Abraham Lincoln Library and Museum at Lincoln
Memorial University, Harrogate, TN

167. **Letter of Prince Gortchacow, Tsarskoe Selo to
"Cher Monsieur Clay"**
June 15, 1862
Abraham Lincoln Library and Museum at Lincoln
Memorial University, Harrogate, TN

168. **Lincoln, Executive Mansion, Washington, to
Hon. Cassius M. Clay**
August 12, 1862
Abraham Lincoln Library and Museum at Lincoln
Memorial University, Harrogate, TN

169. **Cassius M. Clay**
Matthew Brady, ca. 1855-1865
Photograph
Library of Congress

170. **Gustavus V. Fox, Assistant Secretary of the Navy, and His Officers**
1866
Library of Congress

171. **Admiral Nicholas Karlovich Grabbe, St. Petersburg, to Cassius M. Clay**
Paper, sealing wax
January 6, 1865
Abraham Lincoln Library and Museum at Lincoln Memorial University, Harrogate, TN

172. **Mr. and Mrs. Edouard de Stoeckl to Abraham and Mary Todd Lincoln**
June 1, 1861
Letter
Library of Congress

173. **Baron Edouard de Stoeckl**
Matthew Brady, ca. 1855-1865
Photograph
Library of Congress

174. **Banquet Held in Moscow for the U.S. Congressional Delegation, August 25, 1866**
Photograph
After a design by A.C. Savrassoff, ca. 1866
Naval Historical Center

175. **Assistant Secretary of the Navy Gustavus V. Fox with Russian Officers and Officers of USS Miantonomoh and USS Augusta**
1866
Photograph
Naval Historical Center

176. **Sailors on the Russian frigate Osliaba, harbor of Alexandria, VA**
Andrew J. Russell, ca. 1863-1864
Photograph
Library of Congress

177. **The Great Russian Ball at the Grand Academy of Music November 6, 1863**
Winslow Homer, Harper's Weekly, November 21, 1863
Wood engraving
Collection of the American Russian Cultural Cooperation Foundation

178. **Advertisement for photographs of Admiral Lisovski**
Harper's Weekly, November 21, 1863
Collection of the American Russian Cultural Cooperation Foundation

179. **Officers of the frigate Peresviet, Boston**
Photographer unknown, 1863
Naval Historical Center

180. **The Russian Pacific Squadron, Navy Yard, Mare Island, California**
Artist unknown, ca. 1864
Naval Historical Center

181. **The Russian Atlantic Squadron, Boston Common**
Photographer unknown, 1863
Naval Historical Center

182. **Russian Naval Officers**
Matthew Brady, ca. 1863-1864
Photograph
Naval Historical Center

183. **The Russian Fleet in New York Harbor**
Wood engraving
Harper's Weekly, October 17, 1863
Collection of the American Russian Cultural Cooperation Foundation

184. **The Grand Procession of Our Russian Visitors Through Broadway, Under Escort of the Militia and Police**
Wood engraving
Harper's Weekly, October 17, 1863
Collection of the American Russian Cultural Cooperation Foundation

185. **The Russian Corvette Variag**
Photographer unknown, ca. 1863-1864
Naval Historical Center

186. **Rear Admiral S.S. Lisovski**
Matthew Brady, ca. 1863-1864
Photograph
Naval Historical Center

187. **Samovar**
Copper, cast iron, wood
Russia, ca. 1860s
Seward House Museum, Auburn, NY

188. **The Pioneer Boy, or the Early Life of Abraham Lincoln**
Lithograph
J. Mayer & Co., Boston, 1865
Library of Congress

189. **Buoying Vessels Over Shoals**
Abraham Lincoln, U.S. Patent Office, 1850
McLellan Lincoln Collection, John Hay Library, Brown University

190. **Leaf from Lincoln's Sum Book**
Abraham Lincoln, ca. 1824-1826
Library of Congress

191. **Log Cabin of Abraham Lincoln**
Photographer unknown, ca. 1929
Library of Congress

192. **Sarah Bush Lincoln**
Photographer unknown, ca. 1850s
Abraham Lincoln Library and Museum at Lincoln Memorial University, Harrogate, TN

193. **Home of Thomas Lincoln**
I. R. Martin, before 1900
Library of Congress

194. **Boyhood Days of Lincoln (An Evening in the Log Hut)**
Chromolithograph
Eastman Johnson, L. Prang & Co., Boston, 1868
Library of Congress

195. **Cane belonging to Abraham Lincoln**
Wood, ca. 1850-1860
Abraham Lincoln Library and Museum at Lincoln Memorial University, Harrogate, TN

196. **Attention the People!**
1840
McLellan Lincoln Collection, John Hay Library, Brown University

197. **Platter sold by Lincoln in his New Salem store**
Porcelain, ca. 1830
Lincoln College Museum, Lincoln, Illinois

198. **Model of Abraham Lincoln's patent for "Buoying Vessels Over Shoals"**
Wood, ca. 1930
Abraham Lincoln Library and Museum at Lincoln Memorial University, Harrogate, TN

199. **Thomas Lincoln**
Photographer unknown, ca. 1850s
Abraham Lincoln Library and Museum at Lincoln Memorial University, Harrogate, TN

200. **Survey of a Road, Sangamon County, Illinois**
Abraham Lincoln, Michael Killion, and Hugh Armstrong, 1834
Library of Congress

201. **Pounce Box**
Wood, metal, ca. 1847-1857
Abraham Lincoln Library and Museum at Lincoln Memorial University, Harrogate, TN

202. **The National Birth Night Ball**
1848
McLellan Lincoln Collection, John Hay Library, Brown University

203. **Mary Todd Lincoln**
Daguerreotype
Nicholas H. Shepherd, ca. 1846-1847
Library of Congress

204. **A Supplement to the United States Digest**
John Phelps, Little & Brown, Boston 1847
Lincoln College Museum, Lincoln, Illinois

206. **Abraham Lincoln**
Daguerreotype
Nicholas H. Shepherd, ca. 1846-1847
Library of Congress

207. **Fee check for the case of A. Lincoln v. Ill. Central RR Co.**
Aug. 31, 1857
Abraham Lincoln Library and Museum at Lincoln Memorial University, Harrogate, TN

208. **Declaration in the case of John N. Lane &
Willoughby Webb v. John B. Weber**
Abraham Lincoln, July 1839
Abraham Lincoln Library and Museum at Lincoln
Memorial University, Harrogate, TN

209. **Lincoln's Home**
Embroidered portrait
Linen, embroidery thread
National Park Service, Ford's Theatre National
Historic Site

210. **Wide Awake Stovepipe Hat and Ribbon**
Beaver skin, cloth, ca. 1860
The State Museum of Pennsylvania, PA Historical
and Museum Commission

211. **Abraham Lincoln, Cooper Union Photo, 1860**
Matthew Brady, National Photo Company, ca.
1909-1940
Library of Congress

212. **Lincoln-Johnson Political Medallion**
Brass, ferrotype, ca. 1864
The State Museum of Pennsylvania, PA Historical
and Museum Commission

213. **Lincoln Button**
Brass, ca. 1860-1865
The State Museum of Pennsylvania, PA Historical
and Museum Commission

214. **Abraham Lincoln, June 3, 1860**
Alexander Hesler, King V. Hostick, 1956
Library of Congress

215. **Lincoln-Hamlin Campaign Envelope**
S. Raynor, Envelope Manufacturer, New York, ca.
1860
Erie County Historical Society, Erie, PA

216. **Parade Torch**
Wood, metal, ca. 1860
The State Museum of Pennsylvania, PA Historical
and Museum Commission

217. **Lincoln Finial**
Steel, ca. 1860
The State Museum of Pennsylvania, PA Historical
and Museum Commission

218. **Lincoln and Hamlin Campaign Flag**
Linen, ca. 1860
National Park Service, Ford's Theatre National
Historic Site

219. **Lincoln and Johnson Campaign Poster**
Lithograph, ca. 1864
National Park Service, Ford's Theatre National
Historic Site

220. **Wide Awake Candidates Ribbon, Lincoln-
Hamlin**
Silk, ca. 1860
The State Museum of Pennsylvania, PA Historical
and Museum Commission

221. **Abraham Lincoln as Comet or North Star
Envelope**
Samuel C. Upham, Philadelphia, PA, 1861
Erie County Historical Society, Erie, PA

222. **Abraham Lincoln for President Coin**
Brass, ca. 1864
The State Museum of Pennsylvania, PA Historical
and Museum Commission

223. **Wide Awake Man in Parade Regalia**
ca. 1860
The State Museum of Pennsylvania, PA Historical
and Museum Commission

224. **Bill of Fare of the Presidential Inauguration Ball**
1865
McLellan Lincoln Collection, John Hay Library,
Brown University

225. **The National Inaugural Ball Dance Card**
1865
McLellan Lincoln Collection, John Hay Library,
Brown University

226. **Political Debates between the Hon. Abraham Lincoln and the Hon. Stephen A. Douglas**
Follett, Foster, and Company, Columbus, Ohio, 1860
Lincoln College Museum, Lincoln, Illinois

227. **Abraham Lincoln, The President Elect, Receiving His Visitors in the Governor's Room in the State House**
Wood engraving
After a sketch by Henrie Lovie, Frank Leslie's Illustrated News, November 24, 1860
Collection of the American Russian Cultural Cooperation Foundation

228. **Grand Procession of Wide Awakes**
Wood engraving
Harper's Weekly, October 3, 1860
Collection of the American Russian Cultural Cooperation Foundation

229. **Lincoln at Home**
Hand colored lithograph
E.B. and E.C. Kellog, Hartford, Connecticut, 1865
National Park Service, Ford's Theatre National Historic Site

230. **Lincoln's Hammer**
Wood, iron, ca. 1850-1865
Lincoln College Museum, Lincoln, Illinois

231. **Lincoln's Scissors**
Iron, ca. 1850-1865
Lincoln College Museum, Lincoln, Illinois

232. **Mrs. Abraham Lincoln**
Matthew Brady, ca. 1860-1865
Photograph
Library of Congress

233. **Little "Tad" Lincoln**
Photographer unknown, ca. 1902
Photograph, 1860-1865
Library of Congress

234. **Mary Lincoln's Jewelry**
ca. 1861-1865
Lincoln College Museum, Lincoln, Illinois

235. **The President and Mrs. Lincoln at Home**
Calling card, 1864
McLellan Lincoln Collection, John Hay Library, Brown University

236. **Telegram from President Abraham Lincoln to Mrs. Lincoln**
April 28, 1864
National Archives and Records Administration

237. **White House Platter**
Porcelain, ca. 1860
National Park Service, Ford's Theatre National Historic Site

238. **Fido, the Lincoln Family Dog**
Photographer unknown, ca. 1860
Abraham Lincoln Library and Museum at Lincoln Memorial University, Harrogate, TN

239. **Embossed Lincoln Cameo**
Carte de visite
Albumen print, Salisbury, Bro. & Co., Providence, R.I., ca. 1860-1865
Erie County Historical Society, Erie, PA

240. **A. Lincoln to Major General Meade, Army of [the] Potomac**
Letter
November 20, 1863
Abraham Lincoln Library and Museum at Lincoln Memorial University, Harrogate, TN

241. **Union is Dissolved!**
Broadside
The Charleston Mercury, 1860
McLellan Lincoln Collection, John Hay Library, Brown University

242. **Ruins in Richmond, Virginia**
Andrew J. Russell, April 1865
Photograph
Library of Congress

243. **President Lincoln at Antietam, with Allan Pinkerton and Major General John A. McClelland**
Alexander Gardner, October 2, 1863; E. B. Beaton 1907
Photograph
Library of Congress

244. **Gettysburg Address November 19, 1863**
Abraham Lincoln
Collotype, 2000
Library of Congress

245. **Champion Prize Envelopes. Lincoln and Davis in Five Rounds**
T.S. Pierce, J. H. Tingley, New York, 1861
Erie County Historical Society, Erie, PA

246. **Personal seal of President Lincoln**
Sealing wax, paper, ca. 1860-1865
Abraham Lincoln Library and Museum at Lincoln Memorial University, Harrogate, TN

247. **Travel order written by Abraham Lincoln for Major John Hay, July 15, 1861 with Lithograph of Abraham Lincoln and Photograph of John Hay**
Frame containing hand written note of A. Lincoln, lithograph and photograph
Photograph of John Hay, Bierstadt Brothers, New Bedford, MA, ca. 1860.
Collection of The Hon. James W. Symington

248. **Lincoln and His Secretaries, John G. Nicolay and John Hay**
Alexander Gardner, November 8, 1863
Albumen print photograph
Collection of The Hon. James W. Symington

249. **Portrait of Abraham Lincoln**
Michael Angelo Hattes
Oil on board
National Park Service, Ford's Theatre National Historic Site

250. **Lincoln's Hand**
Bronze
Leonard W. Volk, 1886
Collection of The Hon. James W. Symington

251. **The Lincoln Window, Soldiers' and Sailors' Home, Erie, Pennsylvania, 1865**
James R. Steadman, photographer, 2008

252. **Abraham Lincoln**
Mezzotint
William Edgar Marshall, Ticknor and Fields, Boston, 1866
Library of Congress

253. **Portrait of Abraham Lincoln**
Oil on canvas
National Park Service, Ford's Theatre National Historic Site

254. **Contrabands, Newport News**
Alfred Waud, 1861
Drawing on yellow tracing paper
Library of Congress

255. **Abraham Lincoln Writing the Proclamation of Freedom, January 1st, 1863**
Chromolithograph, after David G. Blythe
Ehrgot Fobriger & Co., lithograph, M. Depuy, Pittsburgh, PA, 1864
Library of Congress

256. **Uncle Tom's Cabin, Vol. I & II**
Harriet Beecher Stowe
John P. Jewett & Company, Boston, 1852
Collection of the Silver Swan Company

257. **Abraham Lincoln**
Lithograph
William H. Pratt, ca. 1863
McLellan Lincoln Collection, John Hay Library, Brown University

258. **Coming into the Sanctuary**
Edwin Forbes, Life Studies of the Great Army
Copper-Plate Etching from the series illustrating the Life of the Union Armies During the Late Rebellion
E. Forbes, New York, 1876
Collection of The Hon. James W. Symington

259. **Emancipation Proclamation**
Lithograph
B.B Russell & Co., Boston, 1865
Lincoln College Museum, Lincoln, Illinois

260. **Slave Tags**
Brass, ca. 1840-1865
United States National Slavery Museum

261. **$200 Reward. Five Negro Slaves, Runaway**
September 30, 1847
William Russell, Stylus, 1847
Library of Congress

262. **Slave Shackles**
Iron, ca. 1840-1865
United States National Slavery Museum

263. **Slave Collar**
Iron, leather, ca. 1840-1865
United States National Slavery Museum

264. **Claim for monetary damages in the case of a lost slave, named Goliath**
October 29, 1863
United States National Slavery Museum

265. **Chair made by slaves**
Del Marva Peninsula, ca. 1840-1865
Wood, wicker
United States National Slavery Museum

266. **Dealers in Slaves from Russell's Civil War Photographs**
Andrew J. Russell, ca. 1861-1865
Price, Birch & Co.
Library of Congress

267. **The Four Condemned Conspirators**
Alexander Gardner, July 7, 1865
Photograph
Library of Congress

268. **The Last Portrait of Abraham Lincoln**
Alexander Gardner, February 5, 1865
Photograph
Library of Congress

269. **Satan Tempting Booth to the Murder of the President**
John L. Magee, lithograph, 1865
Library of Congress

270. **Program for Our American Cousin**
April 14, 1865
H. Buckingham and Son, Printers Washington, DC
National Park Service, Ford's Theatre National Historic Site

271. **The Bodies of the Four Conspirators**
Alexander Gardner, July 7, 1865
Photograph
Library of Congress

272. **View of the Box in which the President was Assassinated**
Alfred Waud, April 14, 1865
Drawing
Library of Congress

273. **Bohemian Crystal Toilet Bottle**
Glass, ca. 1860
National Park Service, Ford's Theatre National Historic Site

274. **$100,000 Reward! The Murderer of our late beloved President, Abraham Lincoln, Is Still at Large**
Broadside
Edwin M. Stanton, April 1865
Library of Congress

275. **Lewis Payne**
Alexander Gardner, April 1865
Photograph
Library of Congress

276. **President's Box at Ford's Theatre**
Photographer unknown, April 1865
Library of Congress

277. **Scene at the Deathbed of President Lincoln**
Lithograph
A. B. Ward, Harper's Weekly, April 1865
Collection of The Hon. James W. Symington

278. **Ford's Theatre Ticket**
1865
Abraham Lincoln Library and Museum at Lincoln
Memorial University, Harrogate, TN

279. **Abraham Lincoln's Last Reception**
Lithograph
Anton Honenstein; John Smith, Philadelphia, 1865
National Park Service, Ford's Theatre National
Historic Site

280. **William H. Seward**
Albumen print photograph
Fratelli d'Alessandri, Rome, 1871
Seward House Museum, Auburn, NY

281. **John Wilkes Booth**
Carte de Visite
Albumen print photograph
Silsbee, Case and Company of Boston, ca. 1860
Erie County Historical Society, Erie, PA

282. **Ford's Theatre Orchestra Chair Coupon**
1865
Abraham Lincoln Library and Museum at Lincoln
Memorial University, Harrogate, TN

283. **Flag from Ford's Theatre**
Wool, ca. 1865
Pike County Historical Society

284. **Bohemian Crystal Toilet Bottle**
Glass, ca. 1860
National Park Service, Ford's Theatre National
Historic Site

285. **Silver Catafalque Tassel**
Silver bullion, wood, 1865
National Park Service, Ford's Theatre National
Historic Site

286. **Mourning Ribbon**
Silk, brass, albumen print, 1865
The State Museum of Pennsylvania, PA Historical
and Museum Commission

287. **Mourning Badge**
Brass, albumen print, 1865 The State Museum of
Pennsylvania, PA Historical and Museum
Commission

288. **Death of Lincoln**
Steel engraving
Alexander Hay Ritchie; A. H. Ritchie, New York,
1868
McLellan Lincoln Collection, John Hay Library,
Brown University

289. **Lincoln Memorial. Dissected Leaves**
Photographic print on stereocard
E. & H.T. Anthony & Co., New York, ca. 1865
Erie County Historical Society, Erie, PA

290. **In Memory of Abraham Lincoln**
Mourning card
1865
McLellan Lincoln Collection, John Hay Library,
Brown University

291. **Mourning Envelope**
1865
The State Museum of Pennsylvania, PA Historical
and Museum Commission

292. **Body of the Martyr President, Abraham Lincoln**
Lithograph
Currier & Ives, New York, 1865
Erie County Historical Society, Erie, PA

293. **Mourning Badge**
Celluloid, wigan, satin, wire, 1865
National Park Service, Ford's Theatre National
Historic Site